MODERN
VIDEO MARKETING

Everything you need to know about
using video marketing & content
to grow your business today

FAROUK AJAKAIYE

ACKNOWLEDGMENTS

To my mother, father & 3 older brothers

Thank you for always pouring the best parts
of yourselves into me.
This book and the life experiences it took
to create it wouldn't exist without you.

FREE BONUS GOODIES

Whether you purchased this book, borrowed it, or just happen to be reading the first couple of pages, thank you!

Over time I'll be creating a bunch of free resources that make this book even better.

Videos, worksheets, links to tools, and whatever else people find helpful.

If you'd like access to the extra resources that go along with the book visit **byrouk.com/bookgoodies**

TABLE OF CONTENTS

PREFACE

After reading this book, you will never look at video marketing and content the same again.

First and foremost, it doesn't matter if you plan to read this entire book, skim a few chapters, or just flip through to see if anything catches your attention. Thank you for picking this book up.

If you enjoy this book or think it could help someone else, I hope you share it with a friend or encourage them to get a copy.

Why I wrote this book

Finding out what to do next isn't always easy.

You weigh your options, ask friends for their opinion, wonder if you made the right decision, etc. Well, during January of 2020, I found myself trying to figure out what the next thing I wanted to do was, but I didn't want to jump into anything too quickly.

I'll save you the long story, but after shooting and editing videos for five years and doing marketing work for some of the biggest brands and advertising agencies in the world for eight, I found that at my core, what I enjoyed was creating videos for business purposes.

Sure, creating "lifestyle content" that portrays a fun life can be exciting, but to me, nothing compares to using video in a way that has a positive impact on businesses.

Knowing that using video marketing for business purposes is where I could see myself putting a stake in the ground, I started asking myself a crucial question that any good marketer would, which is, "why would anyone care about this?"

That question got me thinking about not only what I've seen people struggle with when it comes to creating videos for their business but also what I saw online over and over throughout the years.

Questions like:

- *How do I write a script that makes people interested in my product or service?*
- *How can I consistently create video content in a way that makes sense and doesn't feel redundant?*

- *What are some of the unique ways people are using video content & marketing to grow their business today?*

All good questions that led me to wonder who was answering these questions online. As I did more research, I realized that most of the so-called "video marketing advice" online had the same issues. It was either too surface level or a rewrite of one popular video marketing article. Neither of which helps anyone in a tangible way, especially business owners who want to use video to grow.

The biggest thing I realized is that although many people consider using video in their business, there are many barriers & obstacles that pop up and stop them in their tracks.

This book is here to knock down those "barriers" that exist between business owners & using more video content to grow their business.

This book is for you if:

- You know video marketing can do more for your business, but you're not exactly sure of how or where to start

- You're a little nervous when it comes to video marketing and just want to make sure you're approaching it the right way
- You've created a few videos for your business, but you want a more consistent plan
- You want to see if video marketing is for you
- You know everything about video marketing and are actually a spy

Throughout this book, I talk a lot about the "old video mindset" vs. the "new video mindset" that helps business owners and entrepreneurs separate themselves from the competition.

More about that later, but by the end of this book, not only will you have this "new video mindset" that I talk about, but you'll also be able to take action and apply many concepts in this book to your business quickly. Things like:

- Writing scripts that convince people to work with your business,
- Meeting your customers where they are so that your video gets their attention
- How to create quality videos for your business without hiring a videographer.

Those are just a few, but you're in for so much more.

Knowing that this is my first book, I wanted to guarantee you a strong transformation. I intentionally wrote this book in a way that will help you hit the ground running, so there's not much "fluff".

It took me a while to:

- Simplify complex concepts I've learned throughout the years
- Answer the most pressing questions around video marketing, and
- Make all of the information apply to anyone, whether you're just getting started or consider yourself advanced when it comes to video

Although I edited this book repeatedly and had a couple of friends read it for final comments, I didn't go through a big-time editor or waste time chasing a major publishing house. Regardless of those factors, I knew the amount of value this book would provide would be huge, so I focused on packing it full of value and getting it into your hands instead (which I'm sure you don't mind). Sorry writing purists; this book wasn't written to rival the century's greatest writers. It was written to help business owners and operators sooner than later.

I also know that speaking/dictating books is becoming more popular, and there's nothing wrong with it, but I'd like you to know that I wrote every word myself. It meant a lot to me to write out these concepts 100% based on my own knowledge and experiences, which I have been blessed to have a lot of.

At this point, you're probably wondering who the hell I am anyway, so let's dive into my background in case you're curious.

Who I am

My name is Farouk, but most of my friends call me 'rouk for short (which rhymes with Luke).

I am a marketing strategist, brand strategist, and videographer who has had the pleasure of working for some of the world's largest brands and agencies in the world while living in New York City.

I'm lucky to have been able to work on many different projects, meet a lot of different people, and have a lot of different experiences across marketing and branding that have made my experience both broad and deep.

Although I'm notoriously known for not speaking too much about my professional background, here's a summary:

I was introduced to the digital marketing world by my brother Ismail in 2011. We had a website that featured news and commerce all in one place, which wasn't being done as much as it is today. Fast forward to 2013, during my final semester of college at the University of Rhode Island, I was able to convince the Dean of Communications to let me do two concurrent internships instead of taking classes.

I spent the entire semester taking a 3-hour trip back and forth between my hometown of Providence, Rhode Island, and New York City. I had an internship in both cities, and at the time, everything felt so new about New York City that I didn't mind the trip. It felt good to be in the big city. It felt good to be surrounded by that energy after coming from the smallest state.

Fast forward to just one month after I graduated from college, I was able to find a job quickly as a community manager. I worked on the Rolex brand at a small advertising agency called Carrot Creative (now known as Virtue Worldwide) and moved to Brooklyn, New York. Everything was new to me, and I was just learning the ins and outs, but my main mission was to establish my career in NYC.

After Carrot Creative, I was a social media manager at The One Club for Creativity. An international nonprofit organization that seeks to inspire, encourage and develop creative excellence in advertising and design. I had a great time seeing their prestigious award show come together and contributing to their marketing approach the best way I knew how to at the time.

After The One Club, my agency career began, and my life was never the same again. I could talk about this for a while, but below is a quick summary.

To date, I have worked for:

- Ogilvy & Mather as an analyst working on brands like American Express, SAP, Nationwide Insurance, Weight Watchers, and more.
- Havas Worldwide, where I worked on multiple business units under the IBM brand.
- Young & Rubicam (now VMLY&R) as a social media strategist, which is also where I started learning the ins and outs of brand strategy.
- Wunderman Thompson Health as a strategist, working across a few Pfizer and Genentech brands.

Nothing about this trajectory was planned. I just kept doing what felt right. I'm aware that I'm blessed to have experienced this type of career and never take it for granted.

Now, I'm sure all of that sounds great, but let me explain how video came into the picture…

While working for Ogilvy & Mather in 2015, I was looking for a hobby outside of work. Having just a slight interest in the hospitality space at the time, I decided to create a food blog called Beyond The Eats, and my mission was "to share stories and experiences through food." After eating at different restaurants throughout New York City, I realized how much of a thankless job owning a restaurant can be for many, hence the blog's mission.

Anyway, it was time to shoot my first episode. I showed up at the restaurant in Harlem, and on the day of the shoot, the person who was supposed to shoot the video canceled on me. I was embarrassed, apologized to the owner, and swore to myself that it would never happen again. I was still relatively new within my career, living in NYC, and didn't have much money, but about a month later, I bought an affordable camera with some accessories and never looked back.

Fast forward five years of shooting and editing videos for everything from sporting events, tons of restaurants, wedding venues, weddings, threading salons, birthdays, and some other stuff that shall not be specified, and here we are today.

Video is my favorite format to work within by far.

I love it so much that many friends have told me they see the “switch” happen while I’m shooting, and I get “locked-in.” Through a completely unplanned sum of experiences, I’m here today.

Now that you know my story, I’m sure you understand how and why I am writing this book. Although unplanned, my deep marketing and brand-building background mixed with what was just a hobby in video, and here we are today.

In this book, you’ll find a distillation of all of those experiences. Everything I think you need to know and will be useful to you sooner than later.

What you’ll find in this book

Each chapter of this book builds upon the last.

In the first chapter, I start with why you should even care about using video in your business. In the second chapter, I talk about the new video mindset vs. the old one that most people still have.

If you already think you could use some more video in your business, you can skip chapter 1, where I make the case. After chapter 1, I suggest you read the book straight through and don’t skip anything. If you read through in this way, by the end of the book, there is no way that you'll be looking at video content and how you can use it in your business the same.

So, without further ado, flip to chapter 1, so I can explain why you should even care about using more video in your business.

P.S.

There are a few points in this book when I mention old resources that I have, and I would be happy to send them over to you if you reach out to me.

If you're interested, you can find me on:

- Instagram at @itsrouk
- Twitter at @rouk

CHAPTER 1

WHY EVEN CARE ABOUT USING VIDEO TO GROW YOUR BUSINESS?

Nowadays, you can't use your phone for long before seeing video content in some form.

Whether you see videos in your email inbox, on your favorite social media channel, or one of the YouTube videos you watch over and over, video content is everywhere you look. You've probably noticed this shift happen, but for many different reasons, most business owners & entrepreneurs haven't started using video content in a way that will help them grow their business.

Maybe you've tried to get all this video stuff right before but couldn't fully figure it out and gave up. Maybe you've already created videos, but you know you need a better plan. Maybe you're just getting started with all things video-related and want to start strong.

One thing is for sure.

The longer you wait to use video to help grow your business, the more competitive it will get. As someone who's studied marketing over the past ten years and created videos for the past five years, I can let you in on a few secrets.

I talk about some of these things later in this book, but the process of creating video content is only getting more accessible, the adoption of video content is projected to continue increasing, and people are slowly figuring out how to use video content in a way that is beneficial to their business. You don't want to be the last person to show up to the (video) party, and you won't have to after reading this book.

The good news is that if you are reading this, it's likely that you understand that using video content, marketing, or advertising in the right way can transform your business. You just need a roadmap and explanation of how that happens.

Also, just by looking at some statistics, it's clear that investing in video is a smart move:

- 65% of the world's population are visual learners, making video the dominant medium to get your message across.

- Hubspot found that 54% of consumers want to see more video content from a brand or business they support.
- According to Statista, 85% of web users in the U.S. watch online video content, which is expected to accelerate in the months and years ahead.
- According to The Aberdeen Group, companies that use video grow their revenue 49% faster year-over-year than those that don't. They also get 27% higher click-through rates, 34% higher web conversion rates, and 41% more web traffic.

Also, marketers understand the impact that video can have on businesses.

- According to Wyzowl's 5th annual "State of Video Marketing Survey," based on a sample of 613 marketers, 87% of businesses use video as a marketing tool, while 64% of businesses have boosted their use of video content in comparison to the previous year.

As a business owner/operator in the modern-day world, you're operating at a disadvantage if you don't understand how video can help you grow your business.

What makes the opportunity to use video so attractive is that the video creation process has been simplified.

The ease of creating video content, then and now

One big reason businesses are using video content now more than ever is the relative ease of creating high-quality video content. Video used to be seen as a one-off and highly produced piece of content.

It used to be all about getting everything and everyone ready for one video and having one massive production. However, today, we don't have to be that precise. We can take out our smartphone and capture high-quality footage at any moment, which has changed everything… even more than you might realize.

Many business owners still see video for their business as that one highly produced event, which makes sense in specific scenarios. However, approaching video content in this one-off way isn't how most people who are using video to grow their business think about it. If you pay attention to what is working, it's much more about flexibility.

One of the benefits of video is how flexible the format is.

If you're thinking in modern terms, you can have different videos on your website, within your emails, on your social media channels, and even have a live video session where people can watch as you engage with them in real-time.

Having a "modern" approach to video means that you're using video in a meaningful and consistent way, which is essentially the purpose of this book.

Everything I mention in this book applies to your business if:

- You're hoping to get people in your local area to come to your store
- You're trying to sell products
- You want to attract more people to your services
- You want more clients for your coaching/training business

The opportunities to use video to grow your business are truly endless, but you don't have to take my word for it. Let's look at a few examples of how video has significantly and positively impacted a few businesses.

Dollar Shave Club

In March of 2012, Dollar Shave Club helped redefine what it means to use video to generate sales.

Before releasing their now-viral "Our Blades Are F****** Great" video campaign, they were like any other small shaving company looking to make a name for themselves. Thanks to a video that helped redefine their brand, That changed almost overnight. What made it even more impressive is that in 2012, most people didn't use informal humor to sell products and grow their business. You could easily argue that this video paved the way for humor and other unique angles that people use to sell products today.

This one humorous and relatively highly produced video from Dollar Shave Club led to outstanding results as it was one of the first of its kind.

This video:

- Received 4.75 million views in three months
- Generated 12,000 orders within 48 hours of its release
- Crashed the Dollar Shave Club servers due to them being overwhelmed

Stories like these are a little more common in today's world, but more and more, we're learning that people can connect with videos that aren't as highly produced but make the right emotional connection. In fact, we're beginning to see evidence that people are connecting with videos that look less polished much more than they are "professional" ones.

This goes back to what I said a bit earlier about how most people who are getting this video stuff "right" aren't prioritizing a huge production budget. Rebecca Minkoff is one of these people who has found success in using videos that aren't as professional. Over time, she's learned that the most expensive productions don't always lead to sales.

Rebecca Minkoff uses video to increase sales

Rebecca Minkoff is a fashion designer and co-founder of the brand Rebecca Minkoff. The company was founded in 2005 and focused on selling women's clothing.

Throughout the years, she has been able to gain a large following online and use that following to grow the overall brand. As of August 2020, she has:

- Just under 1 million followers on Instagram

- Over 900,000 followers on Twitter
- Nearly 450,000 likes on her Facebook page

Since her brand has been around for years, Rebecca isn't new to using video content to grow it. In an interview with Glossy.co, Rebecca mentioned how she didn't need to use paid advertising to grow the business when she was getting started.

"Somebody asked me what I missed about the early days, and I think it was the organic nature of how things grew," Minkoff said.

"You could cut through the noise without having this big paid strategy. Being part of 'the new thing' gets you a ton of organic press and coverage. It's gotten a lot more expensive to get people to notice you as you grow."

At first, Rebecca's strategy was to try and invest in highly professional and expensive videos, but that approach quickly came to an end after she realized that there wasn't a huge difference in actual sales. She noticed that the videos that were less produced and often shot on her iPhone helped generate sales just as well.

Around this time, she also noticed that her business's Facebook and Instagram advertising costs were rising rapidly, so the company began to move away from those advertising platforms. Focusing on these less highly produced videos was one way for the company to continue to drive their cost to acquire new customers down in a way that made sense.

Although Rebecca wouldn't share exact figures, she mentioned that this tactic, thinking of video in this new and less produced way, helped drive customer acquisition costs down by over 35%.

Although some large brands with existing audiences like Rebecca Minkoff are moving away from paid advertising, many newer brands like Vegamour Skincare are using paid video advertising exclusively to grow their business both affordably and predictably. Let's look at how Vegamour Skincare invests in paid video advertising to grow its business.

Vegmour Skin Care

Vegamour Skin Care launched in 2016, but this four-year-old company has grown quickly by using video advertisements on Facebook & Instagram.

Within the first six months of the brands' existence, they drove $6 million in sales by continuously experimenting with who they were targeting in their advertising and the video content they were producing.

However, as Facebook began limiting access to data & the company grew, they shifted their focus. Instead of using video advertising to get someone to buy one product today, they decided to educate people about their products, raise their awareness, and become lifetime consumers of the product.

Daniel Hodgdon is the founder and CEO of Vegamour. She was quoted saying:

"We slowed down and decided to try and educate our customers about our brand first and see what they are interested in."

Instead of focusing on products, the newer ads educated people on things like the ingredients they used in their products and highlighted that Vegamour is a vegan skincare brand. With this heavy focus on educating customers and increasing subscriptions to their products, Vegamour Skincare has enjoyed lasting success within the highly competitive beauty industry.

More about awareness and how you can raise it later in the book, but their plan for raising awareness was rock solid. They met customers exactly where they were, and it paid off.

Although Vegmaour skincare had a detailed plan for increasing sales, it doesn't always require a plan to "work" when it comes to video content.

Have you ever seen a video tweet, Reel, or TikTok go viral?

I don't have a specific example for this one, but I'm sure you've seen this happen. If not, you'll be able to follow along.

You're scrolling through social media and see this cool product that thousands of people are sharing for one reason or another. Maybe it's something you've never seen before, maybe the product solves a huge problem you have, or maybe the product just looks cool to you. Whatever the reason, you love the video you saw, maybe share it with a friend, and easily imagine how you would use the product/service in your own life.

Let's not forget that somebody posted the video for free, so hypothetically speaking, let's say one of these videos receives about 150,000 views.

Assuming that a lot of people share it because they love the product or find it interesting, that video is almost guaranteed to generate sales due to the number of people interested. Although this happens for different products and brands every day, the key thing to note is that these videos that help generate income were made and posted for free most of the time. The video just did an excellent job of demonstrating how the product can be used and reached the target audience.

I think it's safe to say that you understand why you should care about using video to grow your business.

Still, you're probably wondering something along the lines of how do you get into that mindset of someone who uses video content in a way that helps grow their business? How do you start thinking about video in this "modern" way that I keep blabbering on about?

Let's talk about the new video mindset and how you can get into it.

CHAPTER 2

THE MODERN VIDEO PYRAMID: WHAT SEPARATES THE PEOPLE WHO ARE USING VIDEO MARKETING TO GROW THEIR BUSINESS FROM THE PEOPLE WHO AREN'T

In 1992, Tim Berners-Lee and his team were creating what we know as the world wide web.

In the process of this large project, Tim and a few friends needed a break, so they decided to go watch a comedic musical show titled "Les Horribles Cernettes."

The show featured four female actors and was a smash hit. Tim loved the show so much that he couldn't resist asking the women for a picture. Although they had no clue what the picture was for, they agreed, took the picture, and Tim went back to working on the world wide web.

Little did anyone know at the time, but Tim had a whole new vision for what the world wide web would be. This new vision of what would become the internet included the ability to upload photographs, which is why Tim asked the women for a picture.

This simple picture featuring four women with the words “Les Horribles Cernettes” in glittery red text behind them would technically become the first photograph ever uploaded to the internet back in 1992.

Today, roughly 1.8 billion photos are uploaded to the internet every single day.

Staying ahead of the trend

Let’s imagine that you were on Tim’s team during the making of the world wide web, and you love everything about photos.

Remember, the year is 1992.

You develop your photos. You ask friends for photos; you even flip through magazines and clip them. Since you work with Tim, you understand a little more about his vision and are just hoping to support it, so you start uploading photos you like.

You upload the first few for fun. A month later, you upload a few more, and two months after that, you upload a whole batch that you have been saving. With this habit of uploading photos, you might not know it, but you’re way ahead of the game because people aren’t used to seeing pictures online. You continue to post, and suddenly you notice that you have somewhat of an audience, which only encourages you to post more. Your audience keeps growing; you keep sharing those photos you love, and you feel on top of the world.

But little by little, you notice a change happening. You start seeing other people posting photos too.

At first, you love this change because you can finally connect with other people who love photos!

Even better, these few other people are building an audience of their own too. You continue posting pictures until one day, when you notice a lot more people are posting photos. You start feeling uneasy because a lot of these photos are better than yours. What makes it even worse is that now, you're getting less attention on your website because people are going to other websites and seeing better photos.

Although this is a hypothetical situation, something along its lines was a reality as the internet went from text to photographs. Using photos was a competitive advantage for a while, but that time came and went. Most business owners & entrepreneurs today don't realize that this same thing is happening with video content. That shouldn't surprise anyone because it's just how technology works. It's always out with the old and in with the new, but most people haven't realized how large a shift is happening.

The business owners & entrepreneurs who have noticed this shift are using video to grow their business and reap the rewards. Meanwhile, most haven't acknowledged it, thought much about it, or don't want to coordinate the process (which is understandable).

The mental switch most business owners haven't made (yet)

Video can and should be used to grow your business, support your marketing, reinforce your brand message, and make a genuine connection with your target audience.

I explain how to achieve most of those things within this book, but first, I want to be sure that you understand the difference between the old way of thinking about video in your business and the more modern method driving success.

I spent a lot of time thinking about how to make it easy for you to know if you're using video to the best of your ability and what makes the people/businesses who are doing things "right" different. In thinking about all this,

I realized that assessing the use of video in your business is kind of like a pyramid.

After a couple of bad ideas, I landed on something people seem to love. I call it the Modern Video Marketing Pyramid. I'm excited to explain what this pyramid is and how you can use it to know if you're doing video "right" in your business.

The Modern Video Pyramid

As I've been mentioning, there has been a shift in the use of video for businesses.

While some businesses are using video to grow, others are just slightly or not at all. There is a difference in mindset between these two types of businesses/people, and in this chapter, I'll be explaining the differences to you using the Modern Video Pyramid.

Now, imagine a pyramid with three levels that start at the bottom. In this pyramid, the levels are called:

1. Video Base
2. Video Expansion
3. Video Excellence

Each level of the pyramid has a more robust video marketing plan. Each level helps your business more by using video content more strategically. It's almost always a waste of time to create video content without having a plan for it. Each piece of video content should contribute to a marketing or brand goal that you have in mind, but more about that later in this book.

For now, let's look at exactly how all three levels of the pyramid work.

The bottom of the pyramid: Video Base

What we'll call a "Video Base" lives at the bottom of the pyramid.

These are the foundational videos that most businesses should and usually do have. Although it's better than having nothing, these one-off videos that explain everything about the company are where the video efforts stop. They do all of the "heavy lifting" when presenting your business to new people. These videos are a significant first step into using more video content. Still, they represent the old way of thinking about a video by creating one video and betting everything on it. I call these "foundational" videos because they're the ones that most people who want to learn more about your business will see because they're usually prominently placed.

Here are a few examples of these types of videos:

- **Videos on a website:** Knowing that most people purchase from and learn more about businesses through a website, most brands and companies understand that they need a video on their website's homepage. Knowing that this video will be seen by almost everyone who interacts with their website, most business owners spend a lot of time and money on this one video.
- **Main YouTube page video:** On YouTube, you can choose a "featured video" to show on your channel at the top of the page. The featured video gives you a great chance to make a solid first impression to anyone who visits your YouTube channel. Like a website video, most business owners understand the value of this type of video because many people are likely to see it, and it's in one place.
- **An email welcome video:** Slightly more advanced, but for most online businesses, one of their primary goals is to get new email subscribers who want to engage with their company. After someone signs up for their email list, most people send a welcome email that thanks them for signing up and lets them know what to

> expect. However, sometimes you'll notice that people have a welcome video that you can watch within the email, which can feel like a more direct and impactful message for the person receiving the email.

I want it to be clear that I'm not saying these types of videos are bad. I'm saying that they are just the tip of the iceberg. There is room for improvement if you only have one video in place.

After you get these basics down, it's time to expand!

The middle of the pyramid: Video Expansion

Moving up to the middle of this 3-step pyramid, I have what I like to call "video expansion." What separates this level from the video base is more of a mindset and strategy shift than having specific videos in place.

As I mentioned at the last level, most business owners have no video or just one video on their website and think that's enough. However, there are also business owners who understand how to use video a little more, so occasionally, you'll see them post other videos on social media, in an email, etc. In either case, both business owners could be doing more when marketing their business by creating more videos based on a solid plan.

Businesses in this middle part of the pyramid have what is suggested within the "video base" or know they need these foundational videos. Also, businesses in this part of the pyramid create new content often. They usually understand the importance of using video content but haven't established a plan for exactly how.

If you're reading this book, you might be on the first level, but it's more likely that you're somewhere in this middle tier.

If that sounds like you, you probably haven't realized that you can make it to the next level, to that top of the pyramid where video starts to grow your business and becomes a natural expansion of your business because of it.

Let's look at the top of the pyramid, which I call "Video Excellence."

Video Excellence (& what changed about how we use video)

Finally, we reach the top of the video pyramid, which we'll call Video Excellence.

The business owners & entrepreneurs who are using video content to the best of their ability and seeing great success because of it live in this part of the pyramid.

There's a shift that happened with video content, and everyone in this group knows it.

Before explaining the top of the pyramid, let's quickly look at how the use of video for businesses has transformed.

For roughly the last 75 years, most video-related advertising for businesses has happened through television commercials. For years, companies showed us 30-second commercials for all types of products and services they wanted us to purchase.

The commercials kept going until our technology advanced, then it all happened.

Suddenly, it became easier to hail a taxi cab through apps; it became easier to pay for products through many new payment options; it became easier to order food in minutes. Along with this huge change came more advanced media, and the use of video increased. According to Recode, online video accounted for just 51% of all internet traffic in 2016 but is on track to account for 67% of all online traffic by 2022.

The colossal shift to video changed everything.

It changed things so quickly that business owners were left behind as technology progressed. While business owners understandably focused on their business, video technology advanced. It might seem like you're fully aware of how things changed, but there's a good chance that you missed a couple of things along the way.

Today we use video in a much more natural context.

Taking a quick look at some of the more modern video-related tools available today can help you begin to understand the shift that has truly taken place.

- **Typeform video ask:** Typeform is software that helps you make beautiful forms and collect responses from people in a survey.
  They've released a new product called Video-Ask. This tool allows you to create a quick video, send it to your customers with a question, and receive an answer via text, video, or multiple-choice questions. They refer to this technology as an "almost face-to-face interaction" and show how people use it to generate more leads, engage their audience, recruit people, and get feedback from their audiences. Some people even edit the testimonial videos they get from their customers and use them as marketing materials.

- **Wistia Soapbox:** Wistia is a video hosting platform, and one of its tools is called Soapbox. Soapbox is an extension that connects to the Google Chrome web browser and allows people to record themselves via their webcam or record their screen for a presentation. This enables people to quickly and easily send presentations, create content, do fast outreach via video, and more. It's no doubt that businesses using tools like this have a competitive advantage. They communicate faster and more directly with their audience.
- **Apple Clips App:** Apple's "Clips" phone application helps people create square-sized videos. What's most interesting about the app is that it's made for mobile shooting and publishing specifically. Not only does the app have automatic captions, but you can also do things like include background music, record your video in sections one-by-one, edit the captions, and even add graphics over your video. For creators who are comfortable on camera, a tool like this allows them to create content to post quickly and easily without worrying about too much editing, which is much different from what we have seen in the past.

Using tools and getting comfortable with being informal has become a competitive business advantage for some. If this isn't apparent through today's available tools, it becomes more evident when we look at how real people use video in their business.

An article in Glossy.co that talks about how Rebecca Minkoff has used video to change her business over the years illustrates the point entirely:

> *"After years of testing video, Rebecca Minkoff has settled on a strategy. The company first tried highly-produced, slick video content showing off the product, which didn't move the needle. The video content that drove sales, it found, was raw and personal, shot by Rebecca Minkoff herself on an iPhone."*

We also see influencers being authentic, informal, and keeping what works relatively simple. Sharon Haver, who is a New York City-based Fashion Columnist, Fashion Stylist, and Entrepreneur, was quoted saying:

> *"What sets you apart from anyone else is your own personality. To stand out as a go-to authority, lead with authenticity, have the confidence to truly be you in everything from your branding photos and marketing videos to social media," Sharon*

recommends. "Not only does authenticity elevate the know, like, and trust factor, but it's magnetic to your clients."

What she mentioned is true, but she didn't mention that taking this approach will also help you produce more content. Now, I'm not going to tell you to start making one million videos and not worry about what they look like as many people do, but I will say that waiting for perfection often holds us back for far too long when it comes to video.

Anyway, now that you understand a little more about how businesses are using video in the new context let's jump back into the pyramid.

The best way for me to explain this part of the pyramid is through examples of people doing it right, which should spark a few ideas for doing the same within your own business. These people are so great at what they do that you might recognize their names.

Jubril Agoro

Jubril is a digital marketing entrepreneur who has been making money through different online ventures for years, but more recently, he has seen success by running advertising campaigns for clients.

Years ago, Jubril lived in Chicago and just began to travel the world. However, like many of us, Jubril had dreams beyond his current reality. He was quoted saying, *"I was living in Chicago then, and I realized I could do this anywhere. I wanted to see the world."*

He continued to live his dream of seeing the world until 2016 when once again, he had greater aspirations for his travel endeavors. Jubril had the idea to start Passport Heavy, a video production company created to connect and inspire a new generation of travelers.

This cool YouTube-based video series features destinations worldwide like Mexico, Indonesia, Ghana, Colombia & Brazil. Jubril loves letting his audience know exactly where to go, what to look out for, and what to do around the world.

In return, thousands of people follow and engage with Passport Heavy. As of this writing, they have just under 200,000 YouTube subscribers and 40,000 Instagram followers, proving that there's interest in what Jubril is doing.

Although Jubril always utilizes his Passport Heavy platform, he is often seen in videos on his personal Instagram Story and other social media channels multiple times a week, if not multiple times per day. This gives people the chance to continuously see him, learn a little more about who he is, and see if he is someone they want to see or hear from. It's the small moments like those that we take for granted but could mean so much to the person receiving your message on the other side of the screen.

While Jubril has those base videos we talked about earlier, he frequently shows up in other places with a consistent message, embodying what I call "Video Excellence."

Nowadays, there are many video travel blogs in the same style as Passport Heavy, so you might be wondering what a more "business-specific" use-case might look like. Let's take a look at someone who uses video to grow on one of the most underrated platforms for video today, Linkedin.

Shay Rowbottom

If you're on Linkedin with any regularity, you may have seen a video of Shay Rowbottom.

Part of the reason she's been so successful is that her mindset is a perfect example of people's attitude at the top of the pyramid.

Shay was featured in Forbes, and the article said:

"Her videos seem to pop right off the screen as though she's talking directly to you (because she is). Due to her high engagement and following, they also pop right to the top of your LinkedIn feed."

According to her Linkedin profile, Shay "Turns founders and executives into LinkedIn video creators who are generating massive revenue for their organization."

With thousands of views on every video she posts on Linkedin, a recent feature in Forbes, and an overall personality that shines through the camera, Shay Rowbottom is rewriting the rules for video success on Linkedin. She continuously posts videos that give valuable tips around sales, marketing, and general life advice that has little to do with business. She also does impersonation videos that would make you smile (to say the least).

Although this sounds like an online presence that many strive for, her path wasn't easy. Shay studied viral videos, headlines, and how videos work on the internet for years.

Within the article in Forbes, she said:

"I literally studied viral content for years, worked for some of the largest blogs and brands on Facebook, wrote thousands of headlines, and amassed over a

billion views per month for my clients average during my peak."

It's also common for people to feel too informal when making their videos. Still, like many other people who are consistently producing videos that connect with their audience, Shay thinks the informality of it all is vital:

"A lot of people think that being too open or vulnerable will be a turn-off for business, but it actually just drove more people my way."

When asked what tips Shay would give other people making videos and content for their audience, she provided a clear and straightforward answer in the style that makes so many people love her content.

"Stop introducing yourself. No one cares. Stop trying to sell your solution. No one cares. Start giving free value that would make your target markets' lives easier without asking for anything in return."

Gary Vaynerchuk

If you're reading this and use social media at all, you have likely heard of Gary Vaynerchuk. Although he is a polarizing figure in the online space, and however you might feel about him, not only did Gary use video content to take his life to incredible heights, but he did it all in public.

More commonly known as "Gary V" online, Gary is an Entrepreneur, New York Times best-selling author, CEO of Vaynermedia, and a self-proclaimed serial blueberry eater. If anyone has used video to take their business and life to new heights, it's Gary.

After graduating from college in 1998, Gary took over his father's wine store's day-to-day operations in Springfield, New Jersey. It was called Shoppers Discount Liquors, but Gary immediately changed the name to Wine Library TV.

Along with the store, Gary created a weekly online video series featuring different wines and sharing knowledge with customers. Although it happened slowly, Gary eventually began to amass a large following behind Wine Library TV, and the channel now has over 35,000 subscribers today.

Through clever e-commerce tactics and video, Gary grew his family's liquor store business from $3 million a year to $60 million a year in under five years.

Do you know that massive shift in how some business owners see videos I keep mentioning?

Gary V did more than notice the shift. He led the way by creating a consistent show and hasn't looked back since. After Wine Library TV, his business and personal brands have done nothing but grow.

Now, Gary releases videos on his personal channels nearly every day. His millions of followers across every social media platform prove that what he is doing is working to attract people. Gary has over 8.2 million subscribers on Instagram, 2.5 million on YouTube, 2.1 million on Twitter & 5.1M on Linkedin.

He is excellent at this using video for business stuff and is at the top of the pyramid.

The Modern Video Pyramid

The 3-part Modern Video Pyramid seems simple because it's supposed to be.

Remember, a video that can always represent your business or brand is excellent, but getting that done and moving on to a more consistent way that people can connect with your business through video is the level you should strive for.

Again, I'm not one of those people who think you need to post informal content every day, but I think you should be able to get those "base videos" in place and then post with regularity in a way that helps to grow your business.

Later in this book, I touch on how to post regularly without annoying your audience. However, before that, you must understand how to meet your target audience where they are and how to decide which message you will communicate to them.

Let's talk about meeting your customers where they are and giving them a message that they'll listen to.

CHAPTER 3

WHY USING VIDEO TO MEET YOUR CUSTOMERS WHERE THEY ARE IS KEY, AND HOW TO DO IT

Kenny and Jackie live on two sides of the same coin, but they have no clue.

They both had dreams of owning a cool coffee shop in Brooklyn and happened to be opening their coffee shops in the same week.

When creating the concept for his coffee shop, Kenny focused on offering multiple things people could buy regardless of what they were looking for. Whether you're in a hurry and need a quick coffee, are looking for a tasty pastry, or just want to sit at the coffee shop, Kenny had it covered.

Jackie, on the other hand, had different priorities.

While Kenny focused on providing an extensive range of menu items for every buying scenario, Jackie was focused on her coffee shop being more of a staple within the community and introducing herself to the people who live there. From the decorations to the wellness events to the coffee cups, Jackie focused her coffee shop around the community's ideas, connecting with her customers, and inclusion.

For both of their shops, it was time for the grand opening.

Kenny patiently waited at his coffee shop on the grand opening day, only to attract a few people through the door. The worst part is, most of those people were just asking for directions to the nearest Starbucks.

Meanwhile, Jackie's coffee shop was buzzing.

Groups of people were there talking, meeting each other, and of course, buying coffee. It seemed like Jackie was ecstatic about the opening, but in the back of her mind, she wished she had more items to sell and thought about her customer's needs more. Luckily, Jackie knew that as long as people keep showing up to buy coffee, she would have time to figure out what to offer on the product side.

At this point in the story, you might know where I'm going with this...

To sum it up, while Kenny started thinking about what people will buy, Jackie thought about how she would attract the people she wanted.

Two different approaches, but neither of them are perfect.

Sure, Jackie has some attention, but now she has to scramble to capitalize on it. At the same time, Kenny has no attention, but if he does get some, his wide range of products will be perfect for anyone who walks through the doors of his cafe.

Would you rather be Kenny or Jackie?

The choice is entirely up to you, but in this chapter, I'll show you how you can attract people like Jackie while also being ready to serve them like Kenny through something called a customer journey.

If you don't take the customer journey into consdieration, you're setting yourself up for:

- Having a poor understanding of what content to create and why
- Never genuinely connecting with your target audience
- Having a hard time making your experience better for the customers you have already

I want you to avoid all that, so let's get into what you need to know.

What is a customer journey anyway?

A customer journey is a process that we all go through before we buy things. Sometimes it's a fast process; other times, it takes a while.

The customer journey is a valuable tool for most marketers. It helps you map out all of the interactions and experiences that your customers will have with your business, from finding out about your business to becoming a new and repeated customer.

Depending on who you ask, there are many models of the customer journey that exist. If you're really into this stuff, I encourage you to explore it further on your own, but today, I'm going to teach you about the basics and what you can apply ASAP.

I want you to imagine a horizontal line where the left side is the beginning of the process, and on the right side is the end of it. The customer journey aims to get someone from "awareness," which is on the left, to "retention," which is on the right.

With that said, let's look at what happens throughout each stage of the customer journey.

- **Awareness:** At this step, people don't know who you are, so you want to make them aware that you even exist and what you can do for them.
  In the coffee shop example, Jackie was great at awareness, and Kenny was bad. While Jackie wanted to become known within the community she was now a part of, Kenny was thinking about his offerings. Since Jackie focused on awareness, many people showed up on the first day, even though she didn't have much to offer them.
- **Consideration:** After people know who you are and have some level of interest, they are in the consideration phase. People in this phase are different from the awareness phase because they look for more details about you.
  They want to know more about how you work, what you do, and see if you're the person they want to work with/buy from. In the example of the story, since Jackie focused on the awareness phase, she had a few people out of the many who showed up interested in learning more about her and supporting her. She knew this because they asked questions like how she got started, how they could support her, what else

she planned to offer at the coffee shop, etc. Anyone in this consideration phase has some level of interest, and they just need some information to get them over the hump and into the next step, which is...

- **Conversion:** The 3rd step in this process is conversion. This step is usually everyone's favorite part because it's the step when people spend money. Kenny focused on having tons of products in the coffee shop example, but he had no one to sell to since he didn't think about the awareness or consideration phases. However, if someone did buy from Kenny, it would bring them into the final step, which is...
- **Retention:** Although often overlooked, retention is what you do to keep a customer once you have them. It's cheaper to retain a customer than acquire one, so it makes sense to focus some of your efforts here. In the example of the story, neither thought about this phase. If they did, retention could work in the form of a coffee shop loyalty program where you get one free for every ten coffees you buy. I believe that a TON can be done within this phase for most businesses, but I don't want to go off on a tangent about that, so I digress.

The customer journey becomes even more powerful when you think about using it to make everything better—your social media posts, your videos, your emails, etc.

Since this customer journey exists, and not everyone knows about your brand, it's helpful for you to consider that you're not always speaking to the same person.

Someone who is just learning about you for the first time is different from someone who knows who you are and what you do.

I talk more about this later in the book, and the gears in your mind might be turning already, but knowing that you're making different content for different types of people along this journey brings a sense of relief. It also widens the possibilities and makes your marketing much more targeted across the customer journey.

Even the big brands think about their customer journey and make decisions based on it.

Brie Carere is FedEx's Chief Marketing & Communications Officer. During The 2020 Consumer Electronics Show in Las Vegas, she was asked how she tried to improve the customer experience and said:

"When you think about friction, there are things that are kind of annoying when you're doing your ***customer journey****, and there are things where they can either delight or really piss you off. And we have been measuring all of those,"*

She knows that there is value in improving the customer journey from awareness to retention because it leads to more happy customers. Now that you understand the customer journey, which is powerful if you've never heard of it, let's look at how you can use it to grow your business using video content.

How to use the customer journey to attract new audiences through (video) content

Nowadays, many people in your target audience use video to learn more about your products, services and ultimately work their way through the customer journey. We see these things happen in the form of:

- Unboxing videos
- Product review videos
- Amazon product videos
- etc

Although the customer journey should include all of your interactions with customers across all of your marketing channels like social media, email, paid advertising, and more, today, we'll focus on the video plan for your customer journey.

The key to getting the customer journey "right" is to consider what people think about your business during each journey stage. Not what you want them to think or are hoping they think, but what you know they're thinking already, which is the key to making content that speaks to them from where they are.

As you're about to see, specific types of videos can work for you at each stage of the customer journey and slowly give both strangers and your audience more confidence in your business.

Let's start with awareness videos.

Raising awareness of your business through video

When thinking about what kinds of awareness stage videos to create, it's important to consider what you would say to someone who has never heard of your business before.

This person has never heard of you, never seen you before, and more than likely doesn't care about your brand right now.

Some helpful questions at this stage are:

- What does my business do or provide that would pique a stranger's interest?
- What do I want them to know about my business?
- What's the best way to explain what I do and why I do it to a stranger?

Some popular types of awareness stage videos are:

- **Educational videos:** When someone has never heard of you before, one of the best ways to get them to remember you is by helping them learn something new that they might be interested in. This is why a lot of the free content online encourages you to sign-up, and why many big brands are looking to teach you simple things related to their products & services.
- **Entertaining videos:** Depending on your business, entertaining videos may also work well to raise awareness around your business or brand. Knowing that the person watching the video has never seen or heard of you before, humor is one secret way many people break through the barrier.

- Humor works well because you don't have to care about something for it to make you laugh and keep your attention. After years of working in the marketing world, it's clear that people will always seek humor online (which is a good thing that you can use to your advantage).

Consideration videos

Unlike the awareness level, people in the consideration phase know who you are and are somewhat interested in what you have to offer. Knowing that you already have their attention can help you create a more direct message. Think about how you can create a message that helps to confirm their thinking that your business is one to work with.

Here are a few helpful questions to ask yourself at this stage:

- What do I repeat to people over and over again that suddenly convinces them to buy?
- How can I show testimonials, case studies, or another type of proof in a unique way that gives people confidence?
- Is there a small sample I can give to people that they'll love?

Here are a few popular video types for the consideration phase:

- **Explainer videos:** Have you ever seen those cartoon-style videos that explain a product or service? Thanks to the cartoon style, these videos work exceptionally well in the consideration phase because they explain everything about your product or service in a light-hearted way. Most people love explainer videos because they answer all of the questions in their mind and hopefully confirms their decision to work with your business.
- **Video testimonials:** If people are considering buying from or working with you, you can bet that they will be looking to see if you have testimonials from other happy customers. Video testimonials are criminally overlooked. They provide an even more robust form of proof than a testimonial that is just text. A huge key to getting good video testimonials is showing the transformation that happened after engaging with your product/service. When testimonials are "too good to be true," it's usually because the testimonial didn't show what change occurred due to working with the business or brand, but anyway…

Conversion videos

Congratulations! You've got a new customer, but how do you support them? How do you make them feel seen and appreciated? If you've ever purchased something and felt ignored, especially a major purchase, it's because someone didn't consider conversion along the customer journey.

Although less of a step that leads to a result, the conversion video is necessary because it shows how you follow up. As they say, you only get one chance to make a good first impression.

Two popular conversion phase videos are:

- **Thank you page videos:** When people buy something, having an actual video as a heartfelt message can go a long way. Not only that, but it can also help to communicate your personality so that people will love you even more. Nowadays, we connect with authenticity online, and if you're open to showing it, this is a perfect chance to do that.
- **Email videos:** You've probably experienced what it's like to sign-up for something, then get an email asking to confirm or a thank you. Someone saying "Yes" to you being in their

inbox is another chance to show people that you appreciate their business and say hello by recording a thank you message or even just writing a heartfelt thank you email.

Retention videos

Retention can look different depending on how your business works, but essentially, you want to think about how you can use video content to keep people engaged with you.

Sure, the person has already bought from you, but it costs much more money to acquire new customers than it does to retain them. Think about how you can continue to use video as a touchpoint to keep building a relationship with them, even if it's just quick and informal check-ins.

Most businesses never do this, so it's an easy way to stand out.

If you're selling candles, maybe you give your customers a free guide to choosing candles and candle trends every quarter. If you have a cleaning service, maybe you send a video email and give one of your customers who responds to the video a free cleaning. If you sell online courses, maybe you give away fresh material from the new course you're building along the way.

The goal is to keep the people who already know about you happy, informed about what you're up to, and engaging with you. People often complain about the person who only contacts them when they need something, but the same could be said about businesses.

I can't stress how much the retention phase is often overlooked but can pay off big. I'm sure you have a few ideas based on all of this customer journey stuff already, but before you begin brainstorming (if you haven't already), I want you to know one more crucial thing about the customer journey.

Making sure your customer journey is effective...

You must measure your efforts.

You should be looking at what the numbers tell you and adjust your approach along the way.

Now that you know why an awareness video is different from a retention video, you know that they have completely different "jobs" and speak to different people. Knowing that they have these different jobs, it's important to measure them correctly and not judge them by the same numbers.

As I mentioned earlier, a customer journey is a sum of experiences that people have with your business or brand, so you want to be taking a close look at every step. Be honest about what's working and what's not while still maintaining a certain level of patience.

Now that you understand how the customer journey works and how to meet your customers where they are in the journey, let's talk about the small things in a video that you might never notice but make a massive difference in results.

CHAPTER 4

HOW THE TINIEST CHANGES IN YOUR VIDEO CAN SWAY YOUR RESULTS

Professional British cyclists weren't just bad; they were some of the worst cyclists in the world.

From 1908 to 2003, British cyclists had won just one gold medal at the Olympics. If that's not bad enough, it had been over 110 years since a British cyclist had won the world's most prestigious cycling race, The Tour De France.

British cyclists were so bad that one of the top bike manufacturers in Europe wouldn't sell their bikes to them. They were afraid that their brand would get associated with bad cyclists, and people would stop buying them.

However, things started changing for British cyclists in 2003.

In 2003, the British cycling team hired Dave Brailsford as their new performance director. Dave knew that he had a ton of work to do. He immediately let people know his strategy for turning the team around and turning the British cycling team from losers into winners.

Dave referred to this strategy that would change everything as “the aggregation of marginal gains.” He believed that if you thought about every single thing that makes a cyclist better, from the cyclist themselves to every single component of a bicycle, and tried to make all of those things just 1% better, that you’ll get a significant increase when all of the elements are added up.

After sharing his plan, Dave looked to make 1% improvements on everything.

He adjusted the bike seats for speed and comfort, changed what the cyclists wore after testing different fabrics, studied which products made the cyclists recover faster, and helped each cyclist find their optimal pillow and mattress so that they could get the best night of sleep possible. He even painted the inside of the truck where they kept bikes in all white so that it would be easier to see dust that might be harmful to the bicycles.

Five years after Dave began to make these improvements, everything started to change.

The British cycling team won 60% of the gold medals at the 2008 Olympics in Beijing, China.

However, that was just the beginning of their winning streak.

Four years later, the Olympics came to London, and their team set 9 new Olympic records and seven world records! In 2012, Bradley Wiggins became the first British cyclist to win the Tour De France. The following year, his teammate Chris Froome won the Tour De France and followed it up with wins in 2015, 2016 & 2017.

From 2007 to 2017, British cyclists won 178 championships, 66 Olympic gold medals and won The Tour De France 5 times. With that, the days of people seeing British cyclists as mediocre were over.

Dave understood that these 1% improvements add-up over time and contribute to a larger goal.

The interesting thing is, this same thing happens with the videos we watch. That might sound strange to you (for now), but minor changes we make in the length of a video, its size, how we use sound, and even closed captioning all seem like small choices to make, but become more meaningful choices when they all come together.

In this chapter, I will highlight the things that people think are small choices when making a video but add up to make a huge difference. Without knowing this, you're probably making a ton of tiny mistakes when creating a video that can be easily avoided. Better yet, avoiding them will make your videos significantly more digestible to your audience because you've put a ton of thought into how your audience will receive them.

Let's look at how to make those improvements that add up.

1% improvements: The small considerations that lead to a big difference in how your audience receives your video

Mary Meeker is head of a Venture Capital firm called Bond Capital. Although running Bond Capital takes up a large amount of her time, she's more publicly known for her yearly Internet Trends Report.

This Internet Trends report is every marketer and tech enthusiast's dream.

Every year, Mary highlights the latest trends on the internet through a relatively large amount of detailed slides. In 2020, it had over 300 slides full of insights around how everyone uses the internet and the new habits people are developing. For many people, Mary's insights are a yearly signal of what is to come in terms of how we use the internet.

In the 2020 Internet Trends report, Mary found that of the 453 million hours of video content consumed in May of 2019, 54% was viewed on a mobile device, while 46% was viewed on desktop devices. The report also mentions that 29% of the time that Americans spend watching a video now occurs vertically, compared with just 5% in 2010.

If you're reading this book, these numbers probably don't surprise you much.

If you have any level of interest in using video for business purposes might have realized that video formats are changing. Even YouTube announced vertical video compatibility in July of 2018, signaling a big shift on the horizon.

When you're thinking about creating videos for your business, the format you choose can have a massive impact on how people receive the video and how well your video performs.

Let's look at why the format you choose can have such an enormous impact so that you can make the right decision about the size of your videos.

Vertical, Square, or Landscape

What an aspect ratio is and why it matters

An aspect ratio isn't as intimidating as it might sound at first.

The aspect ratio of an image is simply the ratio of its width to its height.

You usually see it as two numbers with a colon in between, like 16:9, 4:5, or 9:16. If you were saying them in conversation, 16:9 would be "16 by 9".

Each of the popular formats that you see online have an aspect ratio:

- **Vertical videos** have an aspect ratio of 9:16. They are tall videos that are the size of an Instagram or Facebook Story. This format takes up your entire screen if you're on a cellphone, which brings you deeper into the experience of whatever is happening on the video because there's nothing else you can see at the same time or on the sides.
- **Landscape videos** have an aspect ratio of 16:9, and what we're used to seeing on TV. This is also the video format that you typically see on YouTube. I guess you can call this format the

original because it's the main one we've been utilizing for years, and people are most used to seeing video content in this form.

- **Square videos** have an aspect ratio of 1:1. They are the shape of a square and leave black boxes at the top and bottom of the video if you're viewing it on a mobile device. This square size fits perfectly within a typical Instagram post since most posts are turned into a square. One interesting fact to keep in mind about square videos is that they take up 78% more space in a person's mobile newsfeed than landscape videos do, meaning you can see much more of the video on a mobile device.

These are just the more popular sizes, but there are more that people use.

So, how do you figure out which aspect ratio is best?

Now that you have a better idea of what an aspect ratio is, you're probably wondering which aspect ratio is best for your videos.

Although we could guess and do what feels right, it's a much better idea to decide based on what works and look at the data.

Although there isn't too much science behind these formats yet, we do have results that we can look at based on Facebook advertising. When I say Facebook advertising, I mean both Facebook & Instagram.

But why Facebook advertising? You might ask...

Most people don't know that for most social networks', their goal is to keep you on their platform as long as possible. This helps the social network prove that people are actively using it, which gives businesses/advertisers confidence that people will see their advertisements. Knowing that their goal is to keep you on the platform as long as possible, Facebook is known to make the cost of your advertising cheaper if people like the advertisement you have on the platform. They let you know if people like your advertisement through something called a "relevance score" and a couple of other ways.

People being interested in the advertisements they're being shown works out for both sides.

For Facebook, they get to show people advertisements they like, which keeps them on Facebook/Instagram longer. For you, as the person advertising, people are enjoying your advertisement, and Facebook rewards you by making your end-goal more affordable over time.

There are many ways you can tell if online advertising is working or not, but today, I'm going to focus on something called cost-per-click, usually abbreviated to "CPC." CPC is how much it costs you to get each click to the website link of your choice.

Typically, if people don't like your advertisement, this cost goes up. However, if people do like your advertising, the cost will go down.

There can be many other factors into why this number goes up or down, but generally speaking, CPC can be a great general indicator of if an advertisement is performing well or not.

Now that you understand why we even care about CPC, Facebook, or Instagram. Let's take a closer look at what some of the numbers and studies say about which aspect ratio to choose.

The best aspect ratio by the numbers

Agora Pulse is a social media management software, and they have a blog called The Social Media Lab. The Social Media Lab is where they "bust the myths, rumors & stories of social media marketing with science."

They test different hypotheses on social media like:

- "Will Reddit ads beat Instagram ads in the CPC race?"
- "Will overlaid text on Facebook and Instagram image ads Matter?"
- "Comparing long vs. short text captions on Instagram."

One of these tests is titled "Which Video Aspect Ratio is Best for Facebook Video Ads."

To start the experiment they ran 10 tests on different video aspect ratios. 7 out of 10 tests showed that vertical video ads drove an incremental increase in brand lift (which is the number of people who are aware of your brand), including a 3 to 9 point increase in advertising recall (which is the people who remember the advertisement they saw), meaning the vertical/story-sized video advertisement was much more memorable than other sizes.

Knowing this, the people over at the Agora Pulse social media lab wanted to test out square ads (1:1 aspect ratio), vertical ads (9:16 aspect ratio), and regular wide ads (16:9 aspect ratio).

I'll spare you the details of the overall process, you can see all of the details on their blog, but in the end, the results they received were:

- (1:1) Square advertisements: $1.91 CPC
- (9:16) Vertical/Story advertisements: $0.94 CPC
- (16:9) Wide advertisements: $1.79 CPC

If you notice, vertical video advertisements were roughly 47-50% less expensive than square and wide advertisements, although all 3 were the same advertisement, just in a different size!

Let's look at a couple more examples of the difference aspect ratios make.

Buffer is a social media scheduling software that also has a great blog. Like Agora Pulse's Social Media Lab, Buffer is always trying to provide insight into making your "social media game" better.

When it comes to choosing aspect ratios, Buffer has two articles titled:

- "Square vs. Landscape Video – $1.5K Worth of Experiments: Here's How They Compare."
- "Does Vertical Video Make a Difference? We Spent $6,000 on Tests to Find Out".

The second test was run with Animoto, and they both ran experiments to share results. You can find both articles online if you want to go deep into the methodology of the tests, but here's the summary of some of the things they found:

- It costs 7.5% less to get someone to engage with a square video on Facebook and 33% less to get someone to engage with a square video on Instagram.
- For Buffer, their CPC was 26% less expensive with vertical video.
- For Animoto, their CPC was 38% less expensive with vertical video.
- For Buffer, vertical video resulted in 6% more 3-second video views and 187% more people watching at least half of the whole video.
- For Animoto, vertical video resulted in 13% more 3-second video views and 157% more people watching at least half of the whole video.

Across the board and different tests, we consistently see different aspect ratios perform well outside of the landscape version of a video that we're most used to seeing.

Forgetting all of the numbers for a quick second, I want you to ask yourself something that you may have never asked yourself before…

When you see a good video that is square-sized or story-sized and takes up your whole screen, do you feel like you receive it differently?

For most people, I'd assume the answer is a yes. If not, the numbers tell all of the story that you need to know.

As I mentioned earlier and want to highlight, many things can impact a video advertisement's CPC, and more importantly, if and how the video connects with people. To be clear, I'm not suggesting that you go all-in on vertical, square, or any one type of video aspect ratio.

I just want you to think about how you can use these different sizes uniquely, especially when you mix in the customer journey that we learned about in the last chapter.

Now, let's talk about sound.

How sound impacts your video negatively and positively

When people are creating a video, they usually start by saying something about the level of quality.

"Will it be 1080p or 4K?" or "Will this be HD quality?"

I understand why most people start here since it's relatively easy to distinguish low-quality imagery from high-quality imagery. Still, the one place that people tend to overlook that is arguably more important is sound.

Imagine you just got home after a long day, and you're excited to watch that new episode of your favorite show. You get in the door, get comfortable, make a drink and turn on your TV. You turn the show on, excited for all of the crazy things about to happen in the new episode, but you hear a loud background noise similar to an air conditioner frequently. You try and ignore it because you can still hear the character's voices, but man, it's annoying as hell.

After the first few minutes, you decide it's not even worth watching, and you'll come back to it whenever the problem is fixed. Although I doubt your videos would have a large problem like this, you can imagine how annoying the whole experience would be.

Considering sound when it comes to a video can seem simple at the surface, but really, there are three different aspects to sound that impact how your videos are received emotionally, so you need to consider all three.

The three types of sound in a video are:

1. Human voices
2. Background Music
3. Sound Effects

Let's take a closer look at what these three things are and how they impact the videos you make in different ways.

1. Human voice considerations

We use our voices to communicate our ideas and connect, so the human voice being heard clearly can make or break a video for obvious reasons. A study done by Agora Pulse found that videos with subtitles had 7.41% more 30-second views than videos without subtitles on video advertisements.

What this means for your videos is that:

- You should always think about if the person or people you're shooting can be heard clearly.
- You want to make sure your microphone is recording and picking up everything that is being said.
- If you don't have sound, have low sound, or run into any other audio issues, subtitles are necessary.

- If you're recording outside, be mindful of the microphone possibly picking up too much wind and drowning the person's voice.

2. Music Consideration

Have you ever seen a video and felt that the background music was just… way off?

Background music sets the tone for your video and helps to convey emotion. The difference between a soft piano and some hard-hitting rap drums is that you "feel" them in your soul as you hear the sounds. When it comes to making videos, most people understand that music makes a difference and is something most people focus on, so I won't spend too much time here.

What this means for your videos is that:

- You need to pick your background music meaningfully. Are you trying to sell candles? Maybe hard-hitting metal music in the background isn't the best idea (unless it fits your brand… maybe a metal candle line doesn't sound too bad)
- Think about if you want to use music to convey one emotion in the beginning and switch to other music/emotions as the video continues

- Are there any moments when you want to drop the music out altogether? Even if it's just for a second, that moment of silence can be used as a potent tool.

3. Sound Effects Considerations

Last but certainly not least is sound effects.

These are the easiest to overlook because they're not always loud and in your face. Sometimes they're so subtle that you would probably think they're just in the video and weren't purposely placed in.

The difference between having good sound effects and no sound effects is hard to write about, but I think it's something that you should see and hear for yourself if you're interested.

Daniel Schiffer is a filmmaker whose YouTube channel has 1.5 million subscribers. His channel is full of tips, tricks, and more for anyone who creates videos.

He has a video on YouTube titled "One Tip To Dramatically Enhance Your Videos." In this video, he talks about sound design, shows how he adds in sound effects, and most importantly, shows you the difference between a video that has sound effects/sound design vs. one that doesn't.

If you search for sound design, you'll find plenty of examples of what I'm mentioning.

Sound effects are like the underappreciated hero when it comes to making videos, and once you see the difference, you'll never take them for granted again.

What this means is that for your videos, whether you're editing them or someone else is, if there is action happening, it's good to convey the feeling of what you're trying to say by adding the actual sounds around the action.

If someone is skateboarding in your video, how can you add in the sound effect of wheels moving across a pavement? If someone is stirring a cup of tea or coffee, add in that sound of the spoon moving around the inside of a ceramic mug. If someone is eating french fries, how can you add in that subtle crunch sound to make it sound more realistic?

That's what sound effects do.

They take what you're watching and make it that much more realistic by adding a slight element of reality. Sound effects are always something you should think about, whether you're working with an editor or beginning to edit videos yourself.

Now that you understand how sound can positively or negatively impact your videos, let's move on to length.

Video length: Why choosing the right amount of time for your video content is key

When you're getting ready to create a video, how do you choose how long it will be?

While this step is often skipped, and people figure out how long something will be after they have their whole idea, thinking about length can help to create a much more impactful video.

When you set out to create a video, there's usually a goal attached to it.

Whether you're making a video to explain your services and attract clients, a video that shows your product in action, or just a quick video to communicate something with people, when you create a video, there's typically an end-goal in mind.

People overlook the fact that sometimes there's more than one way to get to that goal and using different lengths can help. Sure, the 2-3 minute video that explains what your business is about, who you are, and what working with you is like is important, but have you considered showing people what you do in a shorter format?

For example, let's say you're a personal trainer.

Yes, it's a good idea to talk about your methods for training people, overall philosophies you have, and generally give people an introduction to who you are, but have you considered showing your clients in a 15-second Instagram story that is nicely edited so it stands out? Have you considered condensing your message about how you work with clients into an action-packed 30-second "commercial"? Have you considered getting 1-minute video testimonials and featuring them on your profile? (and you get bonus points if you get them edited to match your brand)

Like many things in life, there's more than one way to reach a goal, and it's the same with video content.

Although we think about video as this one-off or sporadic event, it's better to think about how video can work to promote your business, product, or service in more ways regularly.

If you don't know anything about creating videos, don't worry. Later on in this book, I will walk you through the process of creating your own videos **without** hiring a videographer. You'll be able to produce videos yourself, so nothing is holding you back.

Creating videos without hiring a videographer is one of the most significant roadblocks, so it's something I'm excited to address.

Anyway, more on that later.

For now, I want to talk about one more consideration that adds up when it comes to making videos, which is choosing the type of video you'll make.

Emotion vs. logic, what's the end goal of your video?

Although the technical aspects of creating a video are essential, one of the most important things to know before making a video is your goal.

In brand strategy, two of the critical things a brand must identify are its logical and emotional benefits. Not only what the brand has to offer logically, but the feeling and perceptions that people have emotionally as a result of engaging with your brand.

Knowing your objective will help you decide if the video you create needs to have an emotional or logical appeal to it. Although we often think we must make a rational case to convince people of things, and many times that is true, it has been proven that humans make decisions using emotion first.

Emotion is what makes us feel a connection with people. Emotion is what makes someone see you, your product, or service and say, "that's for me!". Emotion is how people connect before buying anything, and videos that share personality or get people emotionally involved in your business will go a long way for your brand.

This quote from Harvard Business Review sums it up nicely:

"Companies deploying emotional-connection-based strategies and metrics to design, prioritize, and measure the customer experience find that increasing customers' emotional connection drives significant improvements in financial outcomes."

But when marketers create brand stories, they're focused on all the things customers don't care about: ROI, SEO, traffic, brand reputation, etc. And they're gating their content into oblivion. Treating everything they share as if they're classified CIA documents."

However, we can't completely ignore logic.

After someone is interested in working with you, it's logic that will help them make the final decision and take the first step.

Whether that's signing up for an introductory call, visiting your store, or buying your product, people want to know that they're not getting cheated, which is where the logical appeal comes in.

At times, a genuine testimonial video or a video with other proof around your product/service is what people need before making their final decision.

The process of choosing an objective for your video can be relatively straightforward because you probably know what your larger end goal is, but figuring out what to talk about in front of the camera can be difficult.

Throughout the process of producing hundreds of videos, I've seen how difficult it can be to know what to say when the camera turns on. There's something about the camera recording that feels heavy after you press that record button.

Knowing that this is a huge pain point for people, this next chapter is all about my "B-P-S" Bridge system for creating content so that you'll never have to ask, "what should I post?" again.

CHAPTER 5

HOW TO QUICKLY AND EASILY COME UP WITH IDEAS FOR VIDEO CONTENT, EVEN IF YOU DON'T KNOW WHERE TO START

When you're busy managing all of the other parts of your business, consistently creating ideas for your content can be challenging.

Although we know we need a content strategy that we can rely on, more times than not, we post in a way that is sporadic at best.

Although this situation applies to most people, after working with many clients over the years and applying things I've learned, I noticed something...

While we worked together to establish what to talk about, I noticed that we usually stuck to the same few areas. My mind would pull from 3 convenient "buckets" consistently, even though I didn't see it that way at the time. Not only was I pulling from these "buckets" frequently, but they were helping clients achieve their goals, feel confident in the content they deliver, and most importantly, empowered them to think of different ideas for content with ease.

After a while, I felt like I could plug nearly any product or service into this rough framework I had created and instantly get a stream of great content ideas that both the client and I were excited about.

After realizing that this system was helpful, I took a couple of months to think through how I could turn it into more of a process, and the B-P-S Bridge system was born.

The B-P-S Bridge: Use your brand, product, & search to make your video/content marketing efforts successful.

I call this system the B-P-S Bridge because it focuses on the brand, product & what people are searching for around your business.

I call it a bridge because your business is on one side, and the opposite side is your customers.

The "bridge" in the middle is the content you create that will get them from one side of the bridge to the other.

The two reasons why I love this system and think it works so well are:

1. It takes some of the core elements of marketing and brings them to the forefront.
2. It gives you the ability to create multiple pieces of content without coming across as "salesy" or just pushing your product again.

Let's take a closer look at the "B, P & S" within the system and learn how they work together.

B - Your Brand

Your brand is more than your logo or what your marketing looks like.

If your brand strategy is entirely in place, you'll know things like the brands' mission, vision, promise, identity & more. Since a brand is mostly a collection of intangible things, it's easy to minimize the brand we are trying to establish because we are familiar with our brand.

This book isn't about building brands, but brands are a topic I love and have studied deeply over the years. If you want to learn more about building a brand that makes an impact, I'd suggest reading "Obsessed" by Emily Heyward.

If you want to learn more about how to create a brand from scratch, in terms of how to think about it, I highly suggest reading Jasmine Bina's work. Jasmine is the CEO of Concept Bureau, where she does brand strategy for growth-stage startups, established brands, and foreign entities entering the U.S. market. Her podcast and blog posts will give you professional insight into how to build a brand that lasts and connects with your audience.

Anyway, content in this "Brand" category is what you should be talking about that isn't necessarily directly related to your business but your brand.

This is more about the human side of you and what you do, why you do it, and how you do it.

When creating content around your brand, you want to answer questions like:

- What do you want people to know about your product & service at a personal level?
- Why did you get into this business?
- What do you enjoy when you're doing what you do?
- When did you get started, and what has been your experience since?
- What promise do you have, or transformation do you provide to people who engage with your business?

- What values do you take pride in within your business?

I'm sure you get the point.

Assuming you remember what we went over in the chapter about the customer journey, these are usually excellent posts for people in the awareness phase of the journey who don't know you yet. It gives you a chance to tell them about your business and not the products just yet so you don't come off as "salesy."

Now that you understand what the B in B-P-S Bridge is for, let's move on to Products

P — Your product

This is where most people start and end their approach to content ideas. It's the one that I think needs the least amount of explanation because you get it already, but I got your back.

Your product is the thing you want to sell.

If you sell physical products, you will use this bucket to talk about things like:

- Your product proof points
- What makes your product different from the competition?

- What are the main features within your product that you highlight?
- How will the features of this product positively impact the customer's life?
- If you have a sale going on, etc.

If you sell services, this is where you'll talk about what you offer to clients. You would answer things like:

- What your services consist of
- How you deliver your services
- If people can get a special deal now

Use the Product bucket to sell the main thing that your business does, which is likely something you're doing already.

Last but certainly not least is search.

S — Search

- Google processes over 40,000 search queries per second.
- People browse YouTube to learn how to do things and make product decisions, and it's the 2nd largest search engine in the world after Google (who also owns YouTube).

- There are over 1 billion people who use Instagram every month.

The beautiful thing about the internet is that everyone can "choose their own adventure," so to speak.

Unless you're completing a specific task, you're not being forced to visit the websites you do or scroll through your 1,000th (or 2,000th) Instagram post of the day.

Knowing this and having tools that tell us what people are doing while on these platforms is extremely valuable, and where search comes in as the S in the B-P-S.

Talk to any SEO (Search Engine Optimization) expert.

They'll give you recommendations for tools you can use to find out what people are searching for around your business (like answerthepublic.com), so you can answer the most common questions that people have.

I did a quick search within one of these tools for "home workout" to give you an example, and here are some of the results I got back:

- Can home workouts be as effective as a gym?
- What home workout burns the most calories?
- Which home workout is best for weight loss?

These are just a few examples, but there are over 250 results in total!

Most SEO experts suggest using this information to write blog posts that answer the most common questions so that people can find your answer, but what if you used all of the information from searches in a slightly different way?

What if you took all of the questions related to your product or service that people are privately asking in search and turned it into a video? Better yet, what if you took all of the most pressing questions and turned them into an entire video series? You win because you have a bunch of new content, and your customers win because they get answers to questions they either have now or were about to have.

The best part about this bucket is that it's based on research, so you're not guessing where people's interests are and what they want to know. Since video is such a popular format for content across nearly every popular modern-day platform, you can post the content to other channels and have a good chance of answering things for people before they can even ask!

Now that you know what all three letters in the B-P-S stand for let's look at how this all comes together to inform one consistent content plan.

The B-P-S Bridge: How the three parts can work together to give you consistent content ideas

Now that you're aware of the different "buckets" you can pull from, let's take a look at how to draw from them in a way that can develop consistency. Math isn't my strong subject, but luckily we only have to do some simple math here.

Let's say your goal is to post every weekday for one month. Well, using the B-P-S Bridge, the way you'd think of that is…

Twenty days worth of content (5 days a week x 4 weeks = 20 days). I'm going to assume that you want your messages to be balanced, so we'll choose seven things we'll talk about from each bucket, which gives us a total of 21 topics (or days).

After that, you would spread these topics across the calendar, giving you a reliable approach to content.

Although it's a simple example, this way of thinking will allow you to show up consistently and create video content that helps you achieve your business goals. It can be easy to overthink this process and feel like you need a long video every day, but sometimes touching on the smallest points in a shorter video is all you need.

This is slightly advanced, so I don't want to get too into it, but one thing I had to mention is that this system becomes even more powerful once it's used in a video advertising sequence, also known as retargeting.

You may have heard about video retargeting, which is when you can show people videos based on how much of your last video they watched or if they visited your website.

This becomes interesting because it opens the door to doing things like showing people a video about the brand first, helping them through a popular search term second, and if they watched those first two videos, you could finally show them a video of your product.

Again, a lot goes into what I'm describing here, but either way, I hope you have a solid framework for coming up with content ideas, and more importantly, don't forget to have fun.

Your brand is yours for a reason.

Don't be afraid to think of new and unique ways to talk about it, and you definitely don't have to sit there and just talk to the camera. Get creative in how you deliver it!

Now, sometimes you're going to need to make a video that convinces people to buy your product or service in the first place. In that case, as I'm about to show you in the next chapter, you want to answer all of the questions people subtly have in their minds, showing that your business is the right choice.

CHAPTER 6

HOW TO WRITE VIDEO SCRIPTS THAT SELL AND CONVINCE PEOPLE, EVEN IF YOU'RE NOT A GOOD WRITER

Jasmine was excited to tell the world about her new line of skincare products.

She researched for almost a year, carefully created her brand strategy & even told all of her friends and family about it, so they were ready to buy at the launch.

Jasmine was ready to go, and in the process of thinking about marketing, she had an idea to create a video to talk about her products.

She wanted to talk about how she specifically formulated the product for people with combination skin specifically. How the formula featured hyaluronic acid, how she tried hundreds of different products, and how she spent thousands of dollars working through samples before figuring out what works. She wrote a few of these points down but didn't plan anything outside of that because she wanted the video to feel "real & authentic."

Jasmine got her camera and lights set up, took a sip of her coffee, and pressed record.

She stuttered through the first try, but that was expected. She thought the second take was a little better, but she missed a couple of key points. By the third take, Jasmine was beginning to get frustrated because this video wasn't coming to life the way she had imagined. After doing take after take, she figured she would just cut out the parts where she messed up or keep small pieces of what she liked. The problem was that the video had too many cuts and felt too "choppy." Although Jasmine wasn't 100% confident in her final video, she figured it was better than nothing, so she shared it.

Done is better than perfect, but in this story, Jasmine knew she could do better.

Going On Script

If you've ever tried to create a video for your business and wanted to make a script, you're probably familiar with this mindset that Jasmine has. In her case, she still put a video out there, but not knowing what to say when trying to sell a product or service stops many people in their tracks.

Whether you've been in the situation that Jasmine found herself in or not, it's important to know what you're going to say before hitting record so you can get your message across effectively.

I'm about to give you 3 of the only video scripts you'll ever need to sell or convince someone of something through video. After learning how they work, you'll always have a confident and strong jumping-off point for your video scripts.

The three scripts that I cover in this chapter are in order, from the most complicated ones you need to plan for to more simple scripts that are easy to prepare.

I did this intentionally so that you have scripts for every scenario, whether you have months to plan your script or need to think of something in a few minutes.

Use these videos scripts to make customers run to your product or service

Script number 1: The Brain Audit (in video)

Have you ever wondered what is going on in someone's mind before buying from you? How do they make that decision? What turns them on or off? What makes them eager to purchase from you?

This script is a personal favorite and one I use often. My "secret weapon."

I've used this script for a few years now and have seen it produce amazing results both in video advertising and organic video posts. I've noticed that it does a great job of moving people to take action by using how our mind works, which is why I'm here to spill my secret with you today.

Anyway, In Sean D'souza's book The Brain Audit, he talks about the "7 red bags" theory.

The seven red bags theory is a big metaphor for how we think about purchases before we buy things. In the book, Sean paints the picture by using this genius analogy of the airport and making sure you have all of your bags before you leave...

Imagine you just got off the airplane, and you're waiting for your seven bags to come out along the belt. You grab one, wait a little while, grab the second one, and continue to wait for the other five bags to come out. Little by little, you begin to grab your bags.

You grab bags 3, 4, 5, 6, and you realize 7 is taking an unusually long time.

You know for sure that you had seven bags, so of course, you're looking for all 7 of them before you leave. There's no way you're leaving the airport without all seven bags, right?

Well, we also look for seven things before we buy most things, mostly in order, which are:

- A Problem
- A Solution
- A Target profile
- Objections
- Testimonials
- Risk-reversal
- Uniqueness

Let's take a closer look at what is behind each of these 7, how each of these elements work together to convince people, and how this all comes together into an actual script.

I'll be using a fitness coach for this example, but you can apply this script to anything you're selling. It doesn't matter if you run an e-commerce business, are a coach, or have a physical store.

Without further ado, let's start with:

1. A problem

We don't buy most things until we have a problem.

Thinking about our example of a fitness coach, most people hire a fitness coach when they either don't feel confident in how they look or want to take another step forward in maintaining their health.

I'm sure you can already see what "the problem" is all about already.

People wouldn't buy hair products if they didn't want their hair to feel softer, more moisturized, shiny, etc. People wouldn't pay coaches if they could get to where they wanted to be by themselves. People wouldn't pay for cars if they didn't want to use them to get from point A to point B.

There is no desire to buy something without a problem, and this quote from Eugene Schwartz about copywriting sums it up perfectly:

"Copy cannot create desire for a product.

It can only take the hopes, dreams, fears, and desires that already exist in the hearts of millions of people, and focus those already existing desires onto a particular product."

You can not create desire, but you can answer a problem that someone already has and get their attention through the problem.

2. A solution:

After people realize they have a problem, it's on to finding a solution.

One thing to remember about the solution is that people's eagerness to solve their problems varies depending on the size of the problem.

If your stomach hurts, you'll look for ginger or whatever you can get at the pharmacy that helps ASAP. However, if you want a new pair of shoes but already have 50 pairs, you might not feel the urgency to get a new pair.

In the example of the fitness coach, the coach would be the solution to their problem.

I think you get the point here.

People have the problem, recognize it, then begin searching for a solution.

Also, this is more of an FYI, but when thinking about how to speak about your product or service, it can be helpful to get in the habit of mentioning the problem before showing your solution.

3. The target profile:

Although it's not necessarily something people think about, it is a huge part of their consideration of whether they buy from you or not.

Not to be confused with the "target persona," which is popular in marketing and based on the target audience's most common demographics. The target profile aims to serve one specific person who has one particular problem in your audience.

Let's go back to the fitness coach example.

Let's say I'm a man who's in shape but wants to maintain his body. For someone like this, the criteria of who would be the right coach would be different from someone looking to lose 100 pounds.

As someone who's in shape already, maybe I'd look at what type of clients the trainer works with. Are they all relatively in shape? What does their training facility look like? Will I be out of place if I'm the only one who trains hard?

All valid questions, but not something that someone who is trying to lose weight would think.

If someone is looking to lose weight, their questions might be more along the lines of, Can I do this? Has this trainer helped other people lose weight? Will this trainer help me with my diet? I think you get the point.

The target profile speaks to that one "profile" of a person and sticks to it. The main reason is that if one person is having a problem, it's likely that other people have it too. They just need something that speaks directly to them to grab their attention.

4. Objections:

Before we purchase things, there are always objections in the back of our minds. We naturally have objections because we're looking out for ourselves.

No one likes to feel like they bought something they didn't need or is unhelpful to them, so naturally, people have questions before making that final commitment to buying.

In the case of a fitness coach, I might wonder if the person has a good personality and if they'd be able to coach me (because I can get lazy). If they can adjust their coaching style to me, how long will it take me to see results?

Knowing that people always have these objections, you'll want to address them upfront so they can pick up their "red bag" of objections off the airport belt and feel completely confident in buying your product or service.

5. Testimonials:

Nowadays, people have seen so much garbage being sold online. For most people, their guard is way up when buying things from brands they don't know.

One huge way to make people feel more comfortable with your product or service is to use social proof in the form of testimonials. Video testimonials might be one of the most under-utilized marketing tools today.

Not only do people get to hear and see happy clients in video form, but these videos can also be used to create traditional text testimonials that most people are used to seeing. Testimonials or social proof that your business is the "real deal" is a huge "red bag" that people look for. Without it, most people feel like they can't continue moving forward, so make sure you have those testimonials and other forms of social proof in place.

If you do have them in place, and they're done right, your testimonials will help people decide to buy your product or service. I can go on and on about this forever and didn't plan to include this next blurb in this part of the book, but as I write this, I realize it's too valuable for me not to share with you quickly.

Here's a quick piece of advice that I sort of touched on earlier…

Have you seen those testimonials that seem too good to be true? The ones that feel way too perfect? Well, it's usually because they don't show the transformation.

They'll go on and on about the good experiences but never touch on the transformation that occurred or the hard time they had upfront. One quick and easy way to make your testimonials better is to have people talk about the transformation that happened to them as a result of working with you.

Who were they when they started working with you? What happened in between while doing the work? Then, finally, we get to the positives of working with your business.

Again, I honestly slipped this paragraph in at the last second because it's a huge thing people miss, but I would love it if more people knew this.

6. Risk-reversal:

Getting to our last two "bags," risk-reversal, is one of the last things people look for before they decide to make a purchase or inquire with you.

You see risk-reversal a ton when you're checking out for products.

If you've ever seen "guaranteed refund if returned within 30 days!" or "money-back guarantee!" Those are examples of risk-reversal. Risk-reversal is that final piece that makes people think something along the lines of "well if this doesn't work out, there's not much risk anyway. " Although not always 100% necessary, risk-reversal can do a lot of work when it comes to convincing people who are skeptical about working with you.

7. Uniqueness:

Last but certainly not least is uniqueness.

Unknowingly, people are very interested to know what is different about your product or service, and sometimes, that uniqueness can be everything needed to attract people to your business.

The clearest example of uniqueness that comes to mind is a coworking social club in Brooklyn, NY, called The Gentlemen's Factory.

The Gentlemen's Factory, founded by Jeff Lindor, is a coworking social club specifically built for men of color. The Gentlemen's Factory has been featured in publications like The New York Times, Bloomberg, CNN & Business Insider.

In 2019, social clubs were a relatively new concept, but focusing on men of color makes this place extremely unique. (In full disclosure, I am a member of The Gentlemen's Factory.)

In the fitness coach example, one area of uniqueness could be that you only work with people who work 9-5 jobs and need to keep their bodies in shape.

Since you've established this level of uniqueness, and all of your marketing materials speak to this specific type of person, anyone who works a 9-5 job and is looking to keep in shape would take a serious look at you before deciding to work with anyone else.

I could go on about uniqueness forever, but all you need to know is that it's something people look for, whether they realize it or not. Your job is to make sure you subtly place the uniqueness in the right place for them to acknowledge it, which I'm about to show you how to do.

Let's look at how we turn The 7 red bags from The Brain Audit into a killer video script that generates results

If anything about these "7 red bags" is interesting to you, I highly suggest reading The Brain Audit By Sean D'souza. If not, you can continue reading and use what

I'm about to explain to you for the straightforward version.

Anyway, there's a lot that goes into what I'm about to explain, but ideally, you'd start your scriptwriting by speaking to someone who is the target profile for you.

Speaking to this person could and usually does help to find a bunch of new ways to explain your product, talk about what your customers are looking for, and uncover a bunch of insights you would never think of alone.

Speaking to your customers to make your marketing connect with your audience successfully is critical.

If you'd like to learn more about how to speak with your customers to uncover valuable insights, I'd suggest searching through some of Katelyn Bourgoin's work. Katelyn is the CEO of Customer Camp, a marketer by trade, and a "4X founder by choice". Her specialty is "helping marketers and product teams figure out what triggers customers to buy so they can market smarter."

Speaking with customers to start is crucial, which is why it's something I wanted to touch on.

However, the purpose of this chapter is to provide you with a framework for a script that you can use immediately, so let's jump back into the fitness coach example.

Let's pretend I'm a fitness coach who works with 9-5 employees who work in offices. I'll outline everything piece-by-piece before tying the script together at the end so that you can see the thought process behind it.

- The Problem: You want to highlight the problems your target profile faces
    - *Working 40 hours a week in a chair can begin to ruin your body in ways you can't imagine. Your lower back suffers, your movement becomes more limited as you move around less, even your core becomes more weak, but this doesn't have to happen to you.*
- The Solution: You want to introduce your solution, but don't go too far
    - *Hey, my name is Farouk, and I'm a fitness coach who specializes in working with people who work 40 hours a week in an office environment. I've seen the many ways that office work can start to eat at the body, so my fitness programs are designed to stop all of the bad things that can happen.*

- The Target profile: The person you're speaking to
  - *(for this example, we're going to pretend that my target profile was someone I spoke to who works in an office for 40 hours a week but wants to be in good shape. You'll notice I used this information to grab attention in the problem section upfront. Since fitness coaching is something that happens in person, I could get even more specific by mentioning where I do it/my geographical area)*
- Objections: You want to bring any objections up that they might have and answer them. As a hint, many of these are related to time and money.
  - *Before clients begin to work with me, they often wonder whether I can fit their schedule, if they're advanced enough for my program, or if the program makes sense for their specific situation. Well, you'd be happy to know that I keep specific time slots open for my clients who work 9-5, my program has worked with people who have never lifted a weight before, and we start working together after your free*

    - *consultation, where I customize my existing program to fit your body and your goals.*
- Testimonials/social proof: For this part of the script, you want to point to any social proof, testimonials, anything you have that will confirm to people that you're the real deal
    - *If you're hesitant about working with me, head to my website. I have hundreds of video testimonials that feature happy clients who go into all of the details of their experience working with me.*
- Risk-reversal: Although not always necessary, the point is to give people some sort of guarantee if things go wrong or give them a "no-brainer" introductory offer.
    - *Although this isn't something I usually offer, your first session is free if you start working with me within the next two weeks. This will give you a chance to see how I work, how we'll communicate, and if you feel like we're a good fit.*
- Uniqueness: Here, you want to compare what other people do to what you do differently. Help people understand your uniqueness and why it matters.
    - *You can find one million fitness coaches, but finding one that is already aware of the*

> *hurdles you face as a full-time employee is a whole different ball game. Most fitness coaches focus on strength or weight loss, but we'll focus on undoing what the office has done to your body.*

Once we bring this script altogether and make a few edits, so it sounds perfect, what we have is:

> *"Working 40 hours a week in a chair can begin to ruin your body in ways you can't imagine. Your lower back suffers, your movement becomes more limited as you move around less, even your core becomes more weak, but this doesn't have to happen to you.*
>
> *Hey, my name is Farouk, and I'm a fitness coach specializing in working with people who work 40 hours a week in an office or more. I've seen the many ways that office work can start to break the body down, so my fitness programs are designed to stop all of the bad things that can happen to you.*
>
> *Before clients begin to work with me, they often wonder whether I can fit their schedule, if they're advanced enough for my program, or if the program makes sense for their specific situation. Well, you'd be happy to know that I keep specific time*

slots open for my clients who mostly work 9-5 jobs, my program has worked with people who have never lifted a weight before, and we start working together after your free consultation, where I customize my existing program to fit your body and your goals.

If you're hesitant about working with me, I urge you to check out my video testimonials. I have hundreds of video testimonials that feature happy clients who go into all of the details of their experience working with me.

Although this isn't something I usually offer, your first session is free if you start working with me within the next two weeks. This will give you a chance to see how I work, how we'll communicate, and if you feel like we're a good fit.

You can look around for a fitness coach, but finding one that is already aware of the hurdles you face as a full-time employee is a whole different ball game. Most fitness coaches focus on strength or weight loss, but we'll focus on undoing what the office has done to your body with me.

If you're interested in working with me, feel free to email me at....."

And with that, the person has picked up all "7 red bags" and is ready to leave the airport... and by leaving the airport, I mean invest in your product or service.

This is a script that I've seen generate incredible success and is my go-to, so please use it wisely and ethically.

Script number 2: A.I.D.A

Next up, we have the infamous AIDA.

Less complicated than the first script I walked you through and one I know you'll be able to grasp quickly. If you've ever studied copywriting, you've heard of this acronym a ton of times in the past.

AIDA is an acronym that stands for:

- Attention
- Interest
- Desire
- Action

AIDA's concept was created by Elias St. Elmo Lewis, who is in the Advertising Hall of Fame.

In 1898, Elias wrote a column about the advertising principles he found useful throughout his career.

This column he wrote was picked up by The Inland Printer, one of the most popular magazines of the 19th century. He mentioned that all advertisements should follow a specific formula in the column, which is how AIDA's concept came to be. Although he didn't land on the idea of AIDA quickly and easily, the idea evolved and has become a staple within the copywriting world.

I touched on this within the last script, but the first thing you need to know about AIDA is that you must understand your target audience at a granular level for the formula to work.

There's no way to make a script that connects with people if you don't know anything about the person who is in your target audience.

After understanding your audience and hearing from them directly, that's where this script comes in, and I'm sure you'll understand why in a moment.

Attention:

The first thing you want to accomplish is gaining your audience's attention.

This can be done in many ways depending on who your audience is and what they are trying to do, but the name of the game with this script is to grab attention first.

Interest:

After you've earned their attention, it's time to build on it by creating interest. Again, a massive part of this is knowing what your audience is interested in to start, but this step aims to raise that interest level.

Desire:

After you've gained someone's attention and they're interested, it's time to build up their desire and help them see how your product or service can fulfill that desire. This is where you would usually go into more details of what life could be like after engaging with your business.

Action:

Finally, the action is whatever you want people to do to indicate that they want to work with you. Is the first step of working with you a call? Filling out a form? A text? Maybe it's as simple as buying your product, but you're asking the target audience to take action at this stage.

Let's look at an example of this script using the fitness coach angle.

- **Attention**
  - *Do you work a full-time job and have recently had your health fall to the back burner?*
- **Interest**
  - *It's easy to let your health slip when you're working so hard at your job, but don't forget that your health is what allows you to work day in and day out. If you want to stay at peak performance for work, it can be so much easier than you think.*
- **Desire**
  - *My coaching program for full-time employees has taken people who describe themselves as lazy and turned them into people who have more energy, more confidence, and higher performance at work, all due to my simple fitness program.*
- **Action**
  - *If you're a full-time employee who wants to make your health more of a priority, don't hesitate to fill out the free consultation form today. I only have a few spots left this year, so you should fill out the form out sooner than later if you're interested.*

After changing some of the words, so it reads easier and pulling together the complete script, we have:

Do you work a full-time job and notice that you've let your health fall on the back burner?

It's easy to let your health slip when you're working so hard at your job, but don't forget that your health is what allows you to keep working day in and day out. If you want to stay at peak performance for work, it can be so much easier than you think.

My fitness program for full-time employees has taken 9-5 workers who describe themselves as lazy and turned them into people who have more energy, more confidence, and higher performance at work, all due to my simple fitness program.

If you're a full-time employee who wants to make your health more of a priority, don't hesitate to fill out the free consultation form today. I only have a few spots left this year, so you should fill out the form sooner than later if you're interested.

And with that, I'm sure you get the point.

AIDA is a tried and true formula, but people rarely suggest bringing it to a video. Write your AIDA script, record it, and let me know when the results start rolling in.

Script number 3: The who, what, why, how

Finally, the who, what, why, how.

To be honest, this script has saved me in a few situations when I have little to no time to create a script, and I'm sure it will do the same for you.

It's a simple script inspired by Russell Brunson, the founder of a software called Clickfunnels. Although it can and should be planned out when possible, unlike the other scripts, this one can work without a ton of planning.

Although this script is meant to be quick and straightforward, let's quickly break down the different components before pulling the script together, as we did in the last two examples.

- **Who:**
  - Knowing that people watching this might not have any context into who you are whatsoever, this script starts with stating who you are and sometimes how who you are is relevant.
- **What:**
  - The what is when you talk about the thing you're here for today. What is the product or service you're selling? Give it an intro

here, but don't go into too much detail because you want to save that for the next section….

- **Why:**
    - The "why" can be tricky because it can answer several "why's" depending on the situation at hand. Why do they need this now? Why are you the one selling this? Why do they need this at all? The why goes into all the reasons, but ideally, the most important ones.
- **How:**
    - The how is the call-to-action, and when you explain how people can take that first step.

Now that you understand the components let's look at an example using the 9-5 fitness trainer again.

- Who
    - *Hey, my name is Farouk, and I am a fitness coach specializing in helping full-time employees who work in offices keep their bodies in shape.*
- What
    - *Today I wanted to tell you about my coaching program that is now open for a limited time, the full-time fit program. The full-time*

fit program is focused on increasing your daily energy, keeping your body in good shape, and establishing an exercise program to correct your body composition.

- Why
    - *Sitting in your chair or being in the office too much can cause some serious health complications over time. That's why I've decided to focus on this issue through my program. I'm passionate about helping full-time employees achieve optimal bodies for getting work done, so seats in my program are now open.*
- How
    - *If you would like to learn more about me or work with me, head to the consultation page on my website and fill out the form. From there, I'll be in touch within 24 hours.*

After adjusting the script for a little more clarity, here's what we get from the "who, what, why, how" script.

Hey, my name is Farouk, and I am a fitness coach specializing in helping full-time workers keep their bodies in shape.

Today I want to tell you about my coaching program that is now open for a limited time called the full-time fit program. The program is focused on increasing your daily energy, keeping your body in good shape, and establishing an exercise program to correct your body composition.

Sitting in your chair or being in the office too much can cause some serious health complications over time. That's why I've decided to focus on this issue through my new program. I'm passionate about helping full-time employees have optimal bodies for getting work done, so seats in my program are now open.

If you would like to learn more about me or work with me, head to the consultation page on my website and fill out the form. From there, I'll be in touch within 24 hours.

I'm sure you can see why this script works and how you can use it on the fly. If you ever find yourself needing to sell or convince but have no clue what to say, rely on this script.

As I mentioned earlier, the three scripts I just walked you through are in order of most complex to the least, so you're equipped for any situation.

One thing to remember across the board that I can not stress enough is that you need to know your target audience before creating these.

Let's be real.

There's no way you can get someone's attention, as we saw in AIDA, if you don't know what they're interested in. You can't speak to their objections as we saw in The Brain Audit script because you don't know their objections. Connecting with the customer has so many benefits, and I hope I've shown you why.

Now that you'll probably rarely ever wonder what to say in front of the camera again, it's time to take the next massive step in using video to grow your business.

Are you ready to learn how to create quality videos for your business without hiring an expensive videographer or production team?

CHAPTER 7

HOW TO EASILY CREATE VIDEOS FOR YOUR BUSINESS WITHOUT HIRING A VIDEOGRAPHER

Have you ever had a meal from a restaurant that you loved?

One that you loved so much that as soon as you had it, you immediately started thinking about how you could make it at home or modify it?

I'm sure you know the feeling.

If you loved the meal and enjoy cooking, you probably didn't waste a second to take out your smartphone, look up a recipe, and send the recipe to yourself so you can see it later.

After that, you might quickly skim the list to see some of the ingredients, but since you found the recipe, you know that you have step-by-step instructions for how to make this delicious meal that's on your mind.

We often take this approach of "deconstructing" or seeing what different ingredients there are for food, but what if I told you that you could bring that same mindset to creating videos for your business?

At this point, you might be thinking that making a video is much more complicated than putting a recipe together, but is it?

Over the years, many phone apps, physical tools & online resources have made creating quality videos more straightforward.

The problem is, unless you've been creating videos or have an interest in video-related technology, there's no reason for you to explore all of the new video tools that exist.

The only reason I'm aware of the technology is because I've been shooting and editing videos for over six years. As part of my work, and to help my clients get better results, I'm always searching for ways to make better videos with ease.

Over time, I found more and more resources that make creating high-quality videos a breeze, even if I didn't need to use the tool myself. It got to a point where I started telling anyone who would listen... **"you can shoot high-quality videos so easily now!!"**.

In 2018, I even made a free 5-day video course called "Shoot With Your Smartphone."

The course covered how to shoot videos, edit videos, what affordable equipment you need to enhance your videos, and more, using just your smartphone. Although I shared the course with a few people, I never truly put it out into the public. The course is still extremely valuable, so if you'd like access to it, feel free to send me a message on social media somewhere. I include where you can find me at the beginning and end of this book, so don't hesitate.

Anyway, after trying a ton of free and paid phone apps, spending money on some equipment that worked and some that didn't, and using different tools over time, I have found the best way for anyone to create videos for their business at a low cost continuously.

I have to be honest.

This chapter is one that I am extremely excited to share with you because I know you will get a ton out of it! By now, you know that I am passionate about getting more business owners and entrepreneurs to use video to grow their businesses.

People often say, "you don't need anything fancy to make videos," but don't let you know the tools you do need.

So, without further ado, let's talk about exactly what you need to get the job done.

Creating your videos without hiring a videographer

Remember how I talked about "deconstructing" the meal at the restaurant?

Well, before we get into the nitty-gritty, that's exactly what we're going to do, except we're going to do it with videos and not an actual recipe.

There's a lot that goes into each step, but when you break down the process of creating a video, it's just two parts:

1. Shooting the video
2. Editing the video

If you can shoot and edit a video, you've got one complete video.

Simple point at the surface, and of course, there's a lot that happens within each of these two steps, but take a second to think about this as a 2-part process. It will make the process feel less overwhelming.

Anyway, now that we know the two parts of creating a video, the next question is, how do we get those two parts done in a way that is efficient, quality, and helps to get our message across?

To try and keep things simple, let's start with shooting and how you can accomplish capturing high-quality footage all on your own. Capturing your own footage will help you save a ton of money upfront. It's what happens first in the process, so let's tackle that first.

Capturing high-quality footage

If you want to capture high-quality footage, there are two things you need to consider:

1. How you'll record/capture the video
2. The (affordable) tools you'll use to improve your video quality

First, let's focus on how you'll record/capture the video.

When it comes to capturing high-quality footage, there are three main ways you can achieve this:

1. Use your smartphone
2. Use a smaller handheld camera
3. Use an actual DSLR camera

These are in the order of least to most expensive, and if you're reading this book, I can reasonably assume that you own or have access to a smartphone.

Let's take a closer look at what each of these three options consists of.

1. Using your phone

As someone who has created hundreds of videos over the past five years, I was shocked to see what my phone could capture when used right.

The secret was that I just needed a couple of the right tools. Let me explain...

Did you know that your smartphone camera tries to make things "perfect" for you?

I'm sure you take lovely photos, but your smartphone takes many cues from things like the lighting around you and the time of day with every single picture you snap. Although your photos look "natural," the camera on your phone works hard in the background to make the image look good.

If you take a lot of pictures using your phone, you've probably noticed a few times when the camera sees one thing, but what your eye is seeing in real life looks much better. If you've ever adjusted your camera to be more dark or bright right before taking a picture, you know exactly what I'm talking about. Although the photo is ok, you know that adjusting it to be just a little more bright or darker would make it better, so you tinker with it until you find the right fit.

Now, I want you to imagine your phone not having any of these features that automatically “fix” your images for you, but instead, you have complete control over how the image looks.

I won’t get into this too much, but this is precisely why most videographers shoot in “manual mode” instead of automatic. It also allows them to have full control over how the image looks. Things like where they want to focus, how bright or dark the image is, and even making the footage more or less saturated are considerations for the person shooting in manual mode.

Well, there are phone apps that allow you to do the same thing. It might be easy to dismiss a phone app, but what if someone used one of these apps to create an entire film?

Sean Baker is the Director of a film called Tangerine.

In 2005, using an iPhone 5s, Sean and his team shot and edited an entire movie using one of the apps I’m about to share with you. That was back in 2005, so I’ll let you imagine how much better our phones, tools & overall technology are, years later.

The first phone application that became popular for allowing you to shoot videos manually was Mavis Camera. Mavis claims that they're *"the first app to provide professional-level filming tools,"* which gives you an idea of what they were aiming to do when they created this app.

The second app, which I love, was used to shoot the movie Tangerine that I mentioned. It's called Filmic Pro App.

Mavis is free to download and start using, and Filmic Pro is just 15 bucks.

These apps give you camera features like the ability to control your light, see exactly where you're focusing vs. what's blurry, and even give you the option of selecting an exact point to keep and lock focus on. Not only that, but you can also shoot videos in 1080p HD quality, all through the app.

Although there is a slight learning curve, learning how to use these apps can empower you to capture good footage whenever you please.

I started shooting videos with a DSLR camera. However, once I started learning about these apps and using them, my world opened up, and my ability to shoot videos became much more "sporadic" in a good way. I even have many videos that were shot entirely on a phone, but you would never know unless I told you.

Another huge plus to using an app like Filmic Pro is it will teach you the basics of using a DSLR camera in an approachable way. If you're thinking about buying a DSLR camera in the future, this app will help you start learning the ropes.

Learning about these phone apps was a huge turning point for me, and if you're serious about creating videos on your own, it will be a huge turning point for you too.

Although this is the first big step into making videos and all you need to get started on your own, there are a few other affordable tools you'll want to use to take your videos from amateur looking to professional.

Let's look into what some of those tools are.

Making your phone videos shine

If you've ever seen a videographer or video production team in action, one of the first things you'll notice is that they have a whole bunch of stuff with them outside of the cameras. These tools all work together to give whatever video is being created a more polished look.

There are many tools you can use, and over the years, I've tried hundreds of different gadgets, but by far, the three things you should start with and will help you the most are:

- A gimbal
- A phone microphone
- A (small) box light

With these three tools, you'll be able to capture what you need, make it look more professional, and the best part is, none of these tools break the bank. Let's look at how each tool can make your videos that much more professional.

A Gimbal

The first tool I highly recommend is a gimbal.

A gimbal holds your phone and stabilizes it, so you don't have to.

Have you ever seen a video with really shaky footage while someone is walking? Or maybe you've seen the opposite, where the camera is following a person or object closely, but they somehow manage to keep the camera gliding along smoothly. Although they go by a few different names and types, the device is called a gimbal and makes your footage look much more professional since it's a lot less wobbly. You've already read about how small things can add up to what makes or breaks a video in the end, and if the video isn't smooth, it's a little thing we notice.

The second tool I recommend is a microphone.

Fairly obvious, but this one can be easy to overlook if you think the microphone on is enough. Something I learned the hard way in this quick story I'll share with you.

I had a blog called Beyond The Eats, where I share stories & experiences through food. Three years ago, I was at an excellent soup shop in New York City called Good Stock Soups. I was excited to interview Ben, whom I was introduced to by a close friend.

I had planned to do this interview with just my phone, and in the process of setting up, I realized the room was just big enough to create a bit of an echo. I thought it was nothing my phone couldn't handle and wouldn't be a big deal.

Well, you know what happened next.

I had what was probably the worst audio I've ever heard on a video because the echo was so loud. It sounded like Ben spoke into a cup the entire time, and I mean that in the worst way possible.

I bought a clip-on microphone that could attach to my phone the next day and never looked back!

Don't learn the hard way like I did.

Although the microphones on camera are ok, it's a great idea to invest in better audio upfront if you'll be shooting in different environments.

A (small) box light

Last but certainly not least is using a small box light (at least). These small box lights that emit a lot of fluorescent light are a game-changer.

Not only will it help you if you're shooting videos at night and can't rely on just your camera or flash to "see" everything, but you'd be surprised at how dark your surroundings "look" to your camera, while to you, they look outstanding. This is why you see things like ring lights becoming so popular. They add that extra "oomph" to your photos when used correctly.

Although it's not the fanciest solution, your phone can do more than the bare minimum when it comes to making videos for your business.

I started covering shooting with the cellphone example because this is typically the most cost-effective route. However, I assume that you might be looking to invest in a mid-grade camera outside of your phone. If that's the case, you might want to consider using one of the next two options I talk about, a smaller handheld camera or DSLR camera.

2. Using a smaller hand-held camera

In 2007, the Flip camera was launched by Pure Digital and changed everything.

Within the first two years of release, they sold roughly 2 million Flip Cameras.

If you've never seen a Flip camera before, the best way I can describe it to you is like a smartphone, but it was thicker and almost shaped like a brick. The camera featured a small LCD screen on its back so you could see what you were recording in real-time, and it ran on AA batteries. The Flip only shot up to 720p, which was a big deal back in 2009.

I remember this camera fondly because it was lightweight, easy to pull out and start recording, and to be honest, back in those days, having 720p video quality in your hand was a conversation starter.

The future was looking bright for the Flip camera, and then came Cisco…

In 2009, when it seemed like The Pure Digital companies Flip Camera couldn't get any more popular, Cisco purchased Pure Digital for $590 million. Their original vision was to connect the camera to the internet and expand its capabilities. However, this newer idea for the Flip Camera never came to life as the Flip Camera faded away.

Experts say there were many reasons the Flip Camera failed, and among those reasons was smartphone video technology getting better fast. The new iPod was supposed to feature a camera, and the Flip's camera quality wasn't advancing as quickly as the market.

Although one camera's era came to an end, you can argue that the Flip Camera inspired some of today's handheld video camera devices, one of them being the DJI Osmo camera.

DJI Osmo camera

Although the popular Flip camera no longer exists, the idea of a handheld camera packed with features has come back in the form of a few devices, namely the DJI Osmo device and its competitors.

DJI is a Chinese technology company that makes an outstanding line of high-quality video equipment. Within their lineup of many different devices is their DJI Osmo camera. This small handheld camera is packed with some serious features like in-camera stabilization, so videos don't get shaky, an internal microphone, and it can capture footage in quality up to 4K!

This quote from The Verge does a great job of explaining what the DJI Osmo Pocket camera is all about:

"The promise of DJI's Osmo Pocket handheld video camera isn't about giving you the same raw video or audio quality that you would get when recording with a DSLR and an external mic. Instead, this is a camera that prioritizes a simple, compact form factor to help you look much more skillful with a camera than you actually are."

I wanted to mention the DJI Osmo because it's an "in-between" option for capturing video footage.

Assuming you already have a phone that you purchased and don't have a real DSLR camera, this would be a solid option if you wanted to invest in an affordable camera but don't want to break the bank.

However, if you want to invest in a more long-term solution, there's always the option of buying a DSLR camera, whether new or old.

3. Investing in a DSLR camera

When I started creating videos, I received the same advice almost everywhere I looked.

It went something along the lines of "I know you want a fancy camera right now, but to be honest, knowing how to shoot, use light & having good sound are more important."

Something you don't want to hear when you see all of the videos someone is capturing with their fancy camera that costs more than your rent, but it's true.

With that said, if you do have the budget to invest in a great camera, feel free, but there's no shame in having equipment that's a few years old since it's more about what you can do with it.

If you invest in a camera, make sure you factor in the cost to get a good "shotgun microphone", lavalier microphone, lighting, and a couple of lenses. They will do more for your videos than you probably think.

Now that we've covered the different ways you can shoot, we'll move into the second major part of creating videos, which is editing. More about this later, but unlike the shooting portion of creating your video, there are plenty of options for you if you don't want to edit.

Getting your video edited after shooting

Now it's time to turn our attention to the second half of the puzzle - editing.

When it comes to editing, there are two ways you can go outside of doing it yourself:

1. Using "done for you" phone editing apps
2. Hiring an editor

Outside of becoming an editor yourself using Final Cut Pro X, Davinci Resolve, or Adobe Premiere, which are some of the most popular video editing software today, you would use one of the two options above.

Let's take a closer look at how each option works.

4. Using done for you phone editing apps

After you have footage, especially if it was taken on your phone, the option to transfer the footage over to an editing application that will handle the rest can be helpful.

Although the downside is that you can't customize the video to exactly what you're looking for, the plus side is that you can get a decent video made in seconds.

Yes, seconds.

Phone Apps like Quik & Magisto are ones that you should look up if "done for you" apps sound appealing. Apps that let you enter the different video clips you have, and almost magically, get a video created for you, complete with music, transitions, and some text. Although there are likely many more apps that can help you create videos without doing any actual editing on your phone, these are the two I have personally used in the past and recommend to others. In 2021, we're even beginning to see video editing apps that are built for mobile use only.

More about those later, but first, let's talk about Quik.

Quik is a phone application created by the GoPro camera creators. Knowing that it was created to support GoPro footage should hint at what the app was made for. It's easier than ever to capture footage on a GoPro device, upload it to the Quik app, and have a video complete with music, transitions, and more in minutes.

On the Apple app store, Quik's description is:

"With the Quik app, you can create awesome videos with just a few taps. Choose your favorite photos and video clips, then let Quik work its magic. In seconds, it finds great moments, adds beautiful transitions and effects, and syncs everything to the beat of the music.

Customize your story with text and music and easily share it with friends. Editing has never been this fast—or this fun."

Next up, let's talk about Magisto.

Magisto, like Quik, works as easy as entering all of your video footage and photos while the app creates a video out of them. Here's the current description of Magisto on the Apple app store:

"Music Slideshow, Collage & Movie Maker uses advanced Artificial Intelligence technology to find the best parts of your footage and apply video editing techniques including stabilization, object detection, filters, and effects. The result is an eye-catching video that outshines the average slideshow or video collage."

These phone applications might surprise you with how quick and easy it is to create a video, but they might leave you wanting a little more since you can't change smaller details.

In that case, you need a more custom solution.

You need someone who can edit the video to bring your specific vision to life and tailor it to your specific needs, which means you should hire a video editor.

The process of hiring an editor isn't nearly as scary as it sounds; you've got this.

After you do it just once, I have a feeling you'll love it.

When I talk to most people about hiring an editor, they usually have no clue where to start and get overwhelmed pretty quickly. Lucky for you, I'm about to walk you through the entire process step by step and show you how easy it can be.

I firmly believe that hiring an editor for your videos is hugely underutilized for businesses that want to use more video content consistently. As you'll see in a second, there is such a wide range of editors across different price points that video creation in this way should be a "no-brainer" for you.

As someone who's on a mission to help more businesses use video to grow, I'm excited to share exactly how to hire an editor at an affordable price point or even hire a more expensive editor if you please.

Anyway, without further ado, let's get into it!

Hiring an editor for your videos

I'm not sure why, but when I suggest hiring an editor to most people, they think it's much more expensive and complicated than it is.

The reaction always makes me think about one video I watched that changed my whole perspective.

Daniel Schiffer is a YouTube influencer and arguably one of the most talented video producers in the world. One of his YouTube videos is titled "I Paid a Stranger $25 to edit my Pizza Commercial", where he hires people from Fiverr.com to see what their editing skills are like across different price points. If you're considering hiring someone to edit your videos, I highly suggest that you watch it because it will get you excited, and you'll have a better idea of how this all works.

Also, if you've never heard of Fiverr.com, it's a large global freelance marketplace with people who offer a wide range of services at relatively affordable prices.

Anyway, in this video, Daniel partnered with the team at Fiverr.com. He paid different editors on the platform to edit a video based on the footage that he shot, just like you learned how to do in the last section.

He hired a few editors across different price points of:

- $25
- $35
- $75
- $100
- $120
- $275

So he could compare the quality of editing across price points.

While watching this video, you'll quickly notice people who can do anywhere from decent to outstanding work across all of these price points. It ultimately kills the myth that editing has to be extremely expensive to be good, which is why I suggest you watch it and see the results you can get at these price points yourself.

Although Fiverr works, I have also met people who aren't fans of the platform in general or like to invest a little more into another editing solution. If this sounds like you, I suggest you head to another freelance platform called Upwork to find your editor.

Upwork.com is an online global freelance marketplace. The platform has thousands of freelancers worldwide who have different skills across different levels and are ready to work with new people like you. You can find people to hire for all sorts of things on the platform, but we would be looking to hire video editors.

A quick search for "video editor" in the search bar will return thousands of results from across the globe, but you can narrow that search down to the United States if you'd like. From there, you can choose from many different criteria like reviews, their portfolio, etc. To find someone with whom you feel confident.

You can get the criteria down to things like someone outside vs. in the United States, has a certain number of successful jobs they've completed, has made a certain amount of money on the Upwork platform in the past, and more. It will be easy for you to find more expensive/top-tier editors if you wish, and the good news is that a great editor will be able to take your simple footage and make it look incredible.

There are many freelance marketplaces online, and you should feel free to search for other ones. However, between Fiverr.com and Upwork.com, It surprises me that most businesses never use these gigantic global freelance marketplaces to help bring new life to the content that they create.

If you are ready to work with an editor to make this happen, you want to make sure they have all of the details they need to bring your vision to life.

While I worked for big advertising agencies in NYC, we used something called a project brief to answer critical questions around what we were trying to accomplish and why. These project briefs help save a lot of time because they include all of the details around a project, which helps everyone get on the same page quickly by reading through the brief.

It takes a ton of confusion out of projects because everything the people involved need to know is within the brief. People can ask questions about it, adjust it, etc., but everything is in the brief.

Although I won't include all of the elements from a traditional brief, I will give you a few questions you should answer in a document so that your editor knows precisely what you are looking for and you're on the same page.

Creating a (light) brief so that your editor can deliver the perfect video

Knowing that you might be communicating with your video editor through text only, answering these few questions are critical.

Although it will take you about 30-60 minutes to answer these, the time is worth it upfront. Using this time wisely will result in less wasted time communicating exactly what you want over and over again.

Here are a few elements that you should have in your brief:

- Project background
- The ask
- Business objective

- The audience
- Deliverables
- Project Mandatories

Mostly self-explanatory, but I'll quickly touch on each element in case you're unclear.

Project background: The first element of any creative brief is the project background. This communicates precisely what the project is about at a high level and how you got here/why you're looking to get the video created.

The ask: After clarifying the project's background, you want to describe what you're asking for. Not to be confused with the deliverable, where you're more prescriptive with exactly what you need and how many, but the ask goes into more detail about what you're asking for and a little bit of why you're asking for it.

Business objective: Remember the chapter about the customer journey? Whether you're hoping to use this video to raise awareness of what you have going on or generate sales, here is where you talk about the overall business objective. Write about what you would like to achieve with the video you're getting edited.

The audience: After clarifying exactly what you want to accomplish comes the audience. The key to this section is filling out everything you know about your target audience. If you've been in business for a while, you probably have an excellent idea of who buys from you, and this is where you want to share that information.

Like I mentioned in the chapter about scripts, you get extra points for doing actual customer research & getting to know your audience.

Some other questions you can ask are:

- How old is your average customer?
- What do they like to do in their free time?
- Why do they decide to buy from you?
- Do they gravitate towards certain colors?

It might seem like these questions are sort of random, but for someone who has never worked with your business or brand before, it gives them a direct look into exactly who your audience is. It will allow them to apply what you know about your audience to the editing process.

Deliverables: What are you hoping to get delivered?

Whether you agreed on one video, 5, 10, or any other number, you want to be clear on that number and the exact length of the videos you agreed upon. Laying out the deliverables in this way ensures that both you and the video editor know precisely what needs to be delivered, and there's no room for error. You won't ask for three videos and get 1.

Mandatories: Your brand color? Are there timestamps that you want to use? Your Logo in the final 3 seconds? The video must be under 30 seconds?

The mandatories section is where you lay out what is necessary for this project. If the editor gets just one thing right, they should nail everything you have listed in the mandatories section. This section ensures that all of the crucial elements contributing to the video's success are included.

As I mentioned, this is a simplified version of a typical brief, but it will help you get on the same page with your editor.

I'm sure you can already imagine how putting a document like this together will be helpful, but wait until you see it in action. When your editor delivers, and it might take some back and forth to make your vision perfect, the feeling of having a completed video that you can use online is exciting.

With that, you'll have everything you need to create videos, but what's next?

You can just post it to your favorite social media channel, but why not give it a bigger and better job? I like to call it "putting the video to work" for you.

Assuming you have a brand or business that you're serious about, you most likely have 100 bucks to start advertising, and honestly, that's all you need to kick things off.

Let's head to the final chapter, where I'll explain how video advertising works, why you should care, and why you only need $100 to start advertising your business online.

CHAPTER 8

WHY $100 IS ALL YOU NEED TO START VIDEO ADVERTISING FOR YOUR BUSINESS AND ATTRACTING NEW CUSTOMERS

When you hear the word advertising, what's the first thing that comes to mind?

If you're like most people, the word probably has an "icky" feeling to it, and you begin to think of how you dislike them.

However, if you're a modern-day business owner, at the very least, you should understand how advertising works before you decide if it's for you or not.

In any case, one thing is for sure.

Advertising works well for many people and makes them a ton of money. If people weren't making money from advertising, you wouldn't see ads anymore. I will explain more about that later in this chapter, but it's already being proven. Here's a quote from an article that Yahoo Finance published in December of 2020:

"As cable TV subscriptions continue plummeting, digital advertising is growing its dominance as the default medium for companies looking to get eyes in front of their products. Online advertising is expected to reach an incredible $1.08 trillion by 2027."

Now, of course, I'm not here to try and convince you by showing you one quote.

The point of sharing the quote is to help you realize that the advertising market is alive and growing, unlike many people might realize.

The purpose of this chapter is to give you an understanding of how online advertising works and why you don't need a huge budget to get started if you're interested.

If you're already sold on the idea of advertising and know how it works, you're probably ready to go, and this chapter isn't for you. But if not, let's start this off by quickly looking at how advertising online works and why people invest in it.

Money in, more money out: Why invest in advertising anyway?

Assuming you know this, but just to clarify upfront for anyone who might not be familiar, ROI stands for

Return on Investment. You see business owners invest in things like flyers, for example, because people will see the flyer and hopefully walk into their business.

Hypothetically speaking, let's say I print a flyer to promote my business that costs me $2. If 20 people see the flyer I posted in the park, and 2 of them come to my store to buy a $10 product, the return on my investment is $18!

That's a tiny example just so you understand the point I'm trying to make, but sometimes, long-term ROI is why you see big corporations do things like put together big events.

The event reminds people that the corporation exists, which increases the probability that someone purchases from them in the future. Promoting your business will cost you at some level, but companies hope they receive that return on investment (ROI).

When a colossal brand like Coca-Cola buys advertisements, the ones you see over and over and feel like you can't escape, they are hoping to remind you that they exist so that your brain can consider buying Coca-Cola when the time comes.

After you understand how ROI works, I bet you can begin to see how and why this same approach applies to advertising and why it makes sense.

Direct response advertising

Another way that advertising turns into positive ROI is through what is called "direct response" advertising.

This form of advertising was popularized by a man named Lester Wunderman in the 1950s, and to this day, he is known as the pioneer of direct response advertising.

Wunderman believed that the only point of advertising was to get a response back from the potential customer or have them take action, hence the name "direct response."

Many people disagreed with this notion and still do today, but without a doubt, Wunderman changed marketing forever.

Nowadays, online platforms like Facebook, YouTube, Instagram & Amazon allow you to purchase advertising space on their platform. Buying this open advertising space is what helps many people make money online by reaching new people.

All of this sounds great in theory, but you're probably wondering what this might look like in an everyday scenario.

I have a quick story for you to clear things up, but before I jump into it, I have to remind you that the goal of this book is to simplify big and complex topics around video so that you can use the information faster.

A lot goes into advertising the correct way, and it's something I could write a whole separate book about.

Although all of this advertising stuff sounds simple, and I've laid it out in a simple way, all of the fantastic media buyers (which are people who purchase advertising space professionally) that I have worked with throughout the years would kill me if I didn't mention that advertising buying is a skill.

Anyway, on to the story...

Joyce's Candle Store

Joyce finally had her online store up and running.

Although she knew that getting everything set up would be a challenge, she didn't think marketing her store would be hard.

She posted to Instagram and Facebook, told her friends and family about her candles, and even bought small billboards in her town, but nothing seemed to be working. Joyce would sell a few candles a week but nowhere near enough to continue her candle business.

After trying her hardest to make the candles high-quality, picking a name she loved for her brand, and spending more on each candle so that every customer could have a great experience, she couldn't understand why her candles weren't flying off the shelves.

Joyce decided to give her business just two more weeks before calling it quits.

Knowing that her old friend Laticia ran her local farmers market, Joyce thought it was a good idea to try and get a booth there for a day. She gave Laticia a call, and just like an old friend would, she gave Joyce a great location at the farmers market, right next to a man who was selling homemade peach jam.

She thought the man next to her was perfect since they wouldn't compete.

Joyce got to the farmers market, spoke to people all day as they walked by, answered many questions about her product, and even gave one candle away to a man who was extremely skeptical of her product.

Still, she could count the number of candles she sold on one hand.

As Joyce began to pack up for the day, feeling defeated, the man selling his peach jam walked over and started asking her a ton of questions about her candles. After such a long day, Joyce was annoyed at first and thought it was strange but kept answering the man's odd questions.

Little did Joyce know that the more he got his questions answered, the more he loved Joyce's candles. After buying 2 of her candles, which brought her count to 2 hands worth of sales instead of 1, the man pulled out his phone and asked, "what's your Instagram?!"

Joyce shared her Instagram name; the man typed it in and said:

"wow, your Instagram is beautiful! You must be making a killing through Instagram ads".

Joyce wondered why she would ever use Instagram ads and let the man know she didn't have any with a confused look on her face.

Slightly startled, the man immediately started talking about how he could barely keep his peach jam in stock, all thanks to Instagram ads.

"I just do the farmers market on the weekends to meet people and hear what they think about my product, but honestly, about 80% of my sales come from advertising," he said.

Shocked by hearing about his results, Joyce started asking a ton of questions about how it works, if it would work for her, what other types of businesses advertise, etc. After a while, she decided she would give this online advertising stuff a try.

She spent the next few weeks figuring out how all of this online advertising stuff works and even boosted a post or two, but she ultimately decided to hire people who knew more than her. This search led Joyce to an experienced video advertising expert who knew exactly what to do to turn her business around and do all this advertising stuff the right way.

They agreed on all of the specifics of how things would run, learned everything about Joyce's business, and created a group of captivating videos that they would be using for her advertising campaign.

Joyce was still skeptical and didn't fully understand how everything worked, but in the back of her mind, she thought that at very least, if the advertisements didn't work, at least she had some great video content to post.

Joyce couldn't believe what had happened next.

After a week had passed, Joyce noticed a small increase in sales nearly every day.

Although it was slow over the first couple of weeks, she began to notice more and more people buying. The best part was, her cost to acquire new customers was much lower than the price of her candles, meaning her ROI was positive.

Knowing that her CPA (Cost-Per-Acquisition/cost to get a customer) was $15, and each person was spending about $50. It was an easy decision for Joyce to continue advertising and generating more sales. Joyce continued to grow and is now one of the top-grossing candle makers in her region.

If you do a quick Google search, you'll be able to find thousands of stories that are similar to Joyce's. I wanted to share that story to highlight how most people think today vs. how they could be thinking.

Sure, advertising might not be for every business, but most people think of advertising as a bad thing that is only seen in a negative context. Instead, people should see them as an investment that will pay off later and could work for their business too. Of course, the economics have to be right, but that's not too difficult for most businesses, and doing things like having a higher-priced product will help.

Start your journey off in a simple way, with just $100

Although a $100 advertising budget is not much in the grand scheme of things, just knowing that online advertising is an option and trying it out is a huge first step.

To bring all of this into practical terms, if you're looking for a more logical explanation, let's look at some real numbers.

According to WebFX, current CPM's ("Cost Per Mille" is the cost to reach 1,000 people) are just $7.19.

CPM's, let you know how much it costs for your video to be seen 1,000 times, possibly by the same person. If you want to know how many individual people see an advertisement, "Reach" is the metric you would track instead. Anyway, CPM rates change based on many factors, but based on the dollar amount of $7.19, I have a question for you.

Is it worth $7 to have 1,000 chances to get a new customer? Knowing that impressions could count for the same person more than once, is $7 worth 500 opportunities?

Better yet, since this chapter is focused on spending $100, let's stay under $100 and say you spend $93 ($7.19 (CPM) x 13 (1,000 people 13 times) = $93), is

$93 worth 13,000 chances to introduce yourself to a new customer? What about 6,500 chances? I'm sure you get the point.

Again, this is a very high-level explanation.

Results will vary because advertising works like an auction, but to phrase things more simply, would you be open to spending $100 if it means you usually got $200 back? What about $100 if it meant you got $130?

Again, I don't want to make it seem like this is all very easy because people spend hundreds of thousands of dollars per day advertising. There are strategies, tactics, how the auction works, changes, etc. However, now you can consider if advertising is a good route for you to explore.

$100 is just a start, and sales aren't guaranteed, which is why you want to work with someone who has experience. In any case, hopefully, now you understand how advertising works at a high level and why you may or may not want to pursue it.

Although it's not for every business, too many people miss this opportunity simply because they're unaware.

Hopefully, that ends here.

OUTRO

Welcome to the Modern approach to video marketing!

I hope you feel empowered to go out and use video to grow your business.

Although this book isn't backed by a big publishing company & didn't have a team of editors behind it, I'm confident that you've found a ton of useful information in this book.

I hope that sharing the sum of my experiences up to this point has truly helped you feel a new level of empowerment in your business.

Before you close this book, can I ask you for a favor?

Books don't promote themselves, so if you enjoyed this one, I'd really appreciate it if you helped spread the word. Here are a few ways you can help me get the word out:

Share a testimonial: Send a video or written testimonial. You can either @ mention me on social media, or if you have no clue what to write, head to **byrouk.com/booktestimonial**, and I'll have a few questions you can answer.

Snap a photo: Proof that the book is out there in the wild is awesome, so sending a picture of you with the book, the book alone, your dog with it, etc., is fantastic and helpful.

@ mention: I've included where you can find me on social media below. If you want to let me know your thoughts, I'd appreciate it.

I like to use social media to be social, so let's talk! You can find me at:

Instagram: @itsrouk

Twitter: @rouk

Interested in working with me or seeing if we might be a good fit?

Head to **byrouk.com/contact** and we can schedule a time to chat.

Again, thank you so much for reading, and I hope this book helps you achieve incredible new things in your business.

Made in United States
North Haven, CT
07 November 2026

21928339R00099